ONE HEART
WITH
COURAGE

Essays and Stories

info@braughlerbooks.com

Cover and interior illustrations by Julie Lonneman

Printed in the United States of America
Published by Braughler Books LLC., Springboro, Ohio

First printing, 2021

ISBN: 978-1-970063-97-4

Library of Congress Control Number: 2021917438

Ordering information: Special discounts are available on quantity purchases by bookstores, corporations, associations, and others. For details, contact the publisher at:

sales@braughlerbooks.com

or at 937-58-BOOKS

For questions or comments about this book, please write to:

info@braughlerbooks.com

Braughler™
Books
braughlerbooks.com

For the Rizvi men —
Zafar, Qasim and Ali —
with whom I share a journey of the heart.

The author and publisher Braughler Books are donating proceeds from this book to the University of Dayton's Erma Bombeck Writers' Workshop endowment fund, which helps keep the workshop affordable for writers.

Contents

PRELUDE

Prelude

Soon after 2020 dawned, but before the pandemic took hold, I embarked on what Julia Cameron, author of *The Artist's Way*, calls "creative recovery."

I began jotting stream-of-consciousness thoughts in longhand. Not every day. And these short essays were not always very good. That's not the point. The point was to write, to break through whatever was stopping me from creating — whether it was procrastination, fear or laziness.

When all of our lives dramatically changed with the worldwide spread of the coronavirus, I revisited my journal. The opening entry suddenly held more meaning.

To be able to stop time, to freeze moments, what a gift that would be. But as the years race by, the inevitable truths emerge in indelible ink, like "your permanent record" we joke about. Here's what I know now to be true:

So much of life is out of your control. A driver who swerves in front of you. The health scare of a bad mammogram. The unkindness of others. A tornado that uproots trees and lives.

When you feel a lilt in your heart, savor that pure moment of happiness. A connection, a deeply human connection with another person, is magical — and perhaps the best gift life can ever bring. True friendships buoy the spirit and are worth more than anything you can buy. Friendship is priceless. It's to be cherished.

Still, people will alternately fill your heart and break it. The only person you can change is yourself. Accept that.

Life is for living — and every day is a gift. We all need a support system. We are deeply flawed people, living with new hope every day.

Children are spontaneous, not afraid to take risks. They ask you to push them higher and higher on a swing, never afraid of tumbling out. With age, we lose our courage, and it's a quest to regain part of whatever made us feel carefree. There's a time to be practical and a time to throw reason to the wind. The trick is to instinctively know the difference.

When you ask for help, the universe answers. There is a God. Prayers, deeply expressed, help us through the unknown.

Rereading what I had written just months before, I felt thankful that I'd had no idea what 2020 held in store. Who could foresee an extended lockdown that changed our work lives, the crippling fear following a coronavirus diagnosis for a loved one, or a year of political unrest and racial reckoning?

COVID-19 hit home when my husband, Zafar, fought off a mild case. Two tests came back negative for me, yet I battled a mysterious high fever for six days. While I had often thought about compiling my writings for a book, I could never find the time. But as the months of pandemic life stretched toward a year, I thought, *If not now, when?*

At the University of Dayton's Erma Bombeck Writers' Workshop, which I founded in 2000, we encourage writers to quit procrastinating. The three words Erma heard from an English professor on campus are our mantra: "You can write!"

I realized it was time to take those words to heart, with courage. I hope you enjoy these stories and reflections — and find the courage to say "yes!" to the dreams written on your heart.

Teri Rizvi
Spring 2021

I Am From

I am from dog-eared Nancy Drew mysteries
From an endless loop of Herb Alpert and the Tijuana Brass LPs
And my mother's storied meatloaf topped with Heinz catsup.
I am from the sturdy maple tree rising high in the front yard,
The neighbor's patch of winter's frozen water, our version of
    Rockefeller Square —
In a 1950s plat of ranch homes owned by GM workers.

I am from nightly pickup baseball games played in the shadow of
    a water tower
and lightning bugs that danced and dodged our outreached
    Mason jars.
I am from hot fudge sundaes and root beer floats,
Concocted in the family ice cream shop against the backdrop of
    the sun's glorious dip in the evening sky.

I am from "Just wait until you have kids of your own!" and
    "Because I said so!"
And from "Olly Olly Oxen Free," the sing-song chant of hide-and-
    seek games.
I am from summer pilgrimages to Hot Springs, Arkansas, in the
    family station wagon
And jaunts up the road to watch Johnny Bench and Tony Perez
    slug the ball.
I am from tradition — the turntable spinning Bing Crosby's
    "Silver Bells,"

The aroma of roast duck and sauerkraut on New Year's Day,

The donning of Easter bonnets and dapper hats, four siblings
    awkwardly lined up for a family photo by the Impala.

I am from the heartland

Where summer rains soak that majestic maple tree of
    my childhood,

Its branches stretching skyward in hope, its deep roots grounded
    in faith.

(Summer 2019)

COURAGE

Sowing Hope

Instead of sitting in a crowded New York Yankees stadium, we hung out in our family room more than 600 miles away and watched Ali's graduation from NYU's Silver School of Social Work play out on the TV screen.

Perched on the couch, our son wore his NYU graduation cap and high school gown, coincidentally the perfect hue of purple. My eyes glistened with unexpected tears.

Dean Neil B. Guterman's words to the graduating class felt prophetic: "Out of crisis are the seeds of change, the seeds of transformation, the seeds of growth, the seeds of healing and advancing compassion and social justice. That's what social work is all about. It's taking the most difficult situation and finding the opportunity for elevation."

The pandemic has forced us to up our game, dipping into a well of resiliency, vulnerability and courage in the face of an unknown — but now more hopeful — future with vaccines slowly being rolled out. For all we've lost during these lost days, we've gained in wisdom.

And, for Ali, wisdom beyond a piece of parchment.

"I'm going back to New York in a week," he told me when he arrived home for spring break in March. "You don't understand; I'm in a relationship." He was unaware that it would not be safe enough to return until after Father's Day.

With airlines grounded and New York City in lockdown, his last semester of graduate classes moved to Zoom rooms. From the patio, I watched him silhouetted in his childhood bedroom window as he donned headphones and participated in remote classes. His emotionally challenging fieldwork as a mental health counselor at Rikers Island fell to the wayside and his licensing exam was postponed, like so many of his plans on the journey to graduation.

Meanwhile, in his adopted city, hospitals arranged temporary morgues, set to the incongruous soundtrack of wailing ambulance sirens and New Yorkers singing the Beatles' "Yellow Submarine" and other nightly songs with one another from their apartment windows. In despair, always hope.

Still, life had thrown a curveball to my son. Time stretched out like an endless country road, slicked with rain, begging him to slow down. Like a contemporary Thoreau, he retreated to the woods behind our house to learn lessons not found in a textbook.

The cold March air filled with the whirring of a chainsaw as he cut through a quarter-century of neglect with the precision of a Swiss watchmaker. He hooked a wagon to the riding mower and brought chopped logs out of the crevices of the forest, carefully stacking them for firewood. He burned the brush and cut a path through the weed-choked acres, creating a natural oasis of tranquility.

By night, he experimented in the kitchen, throwing a medley of spices in a rice, tofu and vegetable dish as we shared recipes and conversed about his dreams. He arranged a Zoom cooking date with his girlfriend quarantining with her family in Florida, went on socially distanced walks with a friend, taught himself to embroider and flew a kite in the outstretched front yard. Part of the colorful kite and tail remain stuck on a high tree branch, gently blowing in the distance in a symbolic dance. Like the tree's boughs, the pandemic will eventually release its grasp.

March turned into April, then into May. A Black man died

under the knee of a white police officer, sparking the greatest civil unrest since the 1960s. A president downplayed a virus that has now taken hundreds of thousands of lives, disproportionately the elderly and the poor. A deeply divided, broken nation turned on itself, reminding us how fragile life can be in the face of uncertainty and fear.

Against this cacophony, Ali planted sunflowers, blueberry bushes, tomatoes — and 50 tiny fir trees deep in the woods. Planting a tree is a show of faith in the future.

Then he returned to Brooklyn, where he has carved out a new life counseling HIV-positive adults, many of whom have faced homelessness. Always a gardener, he's scattering seeds of healing and transformation.

With every seed, the promise of new life.

(Winter 2020)

Our Fault

As my son Ali pulls out of the driveway in a rented Dodge Caravan loaded with a mattress, his favorite clothes, a few plants and a "Protect the Children" sign from this spring's gun violence protest in Washington, D.C., my eyes brim with tears.

It's not that I will go all that long without seeing him. Later that week in New York City, his father and I will tour his multi-ethnic, largely Spanish-speaking Harlem neighborhood along the Hudson River. Here's where he'll live and work while pursuing a master's degree in social work a subway ride and a world away at NYU.

A world away from us.

I hear the echoes of Ali's words, offered playfully at a family dinner the summer before this departure: "This is all your fault, really. You raised me to be a global citizen."

He reminded us of our lives in our 20s, and he had a point. Fresh out of journalism school at 22, exactly Ali's age, I jumped on an overnight standby Air India flight to London with my two college roommates for a $150-a-week internship with McGraw-Hill World News. I had a job, but no place to live. My adventurous friends had neither. Through the prism of youth, we viewed life as a grand adventure, not a mystery to be solved. We wore our idealism in those days like a cherished sweater.

As for his father, today he is a CEO, but back then, he was a rebel by anyone's standard. With a passport he received just days earlier, Zafar left his close-knit family, hopped in a car with a cousin and two friends and drove from Lahore, Pakistan, to

Tehran, Iran, where the car broke down. Undaunted, the three hopped a train to Istanbul, then another one to Munich, then one more to the Strait of Dover for a ferry to England. No plan, no student visa, little money — just the possibility of a new life stretching as far as the North Sea. That impromptu visit to a foreign land turned into a seven-year stay in London filled with classes, accounting jobs, adventures and, finally, me — the one he followed to the U.S.

Now our own son was venturing into the unknown with little more than a monthly subway pass, the audacity of youth and, admittedly, some trepidation. After all, he is not a city person at heart. His roots are so strong in his tiny hometown of Vandalia, Ohio, that the local coffee shop tacked up a "Wanted" poster with his "mug shot" and a reward of 500 coffee beans when he left for college just a dozen miles away.

Yet when someone you respect believes in you, it can rock your world and expand your horizons. He discovered that for himself at the University of Dayton, where professors Margaret Strain and Lori Phillips-Young left their office doors open for him, taking time for long chats about the monumental and the mundane, always encouraging him to live his best life. He spent part of a summer in Zambia living among village children. By his senior year, he was sharing a three-story student house with nine roommates, some of whom became like brothers.

After graduation, he became a teacher in the Miracle Makers summer program at Dayton's inner-city Ruskin Elementary School. As he neared his final day, he wrote each student a parting letter filled with pride in their achievements, belief in their dreams and gratitude "for teaching me as much as I have taught you." They cried. He wept.

It's never easy leaving family, treasured friends and the

reassuring rituals of the familiar, but we rarely expand the boundaries of our world unless we venture outside that comfort zone.

A text from Ali came in at the end of our weekend visit, as we waited to board our return flight to Dayton. It said, "Change is usually good." When I reluctantly agreed, he quickly texted, "Again, your fault."

Sigh.

We raise our children to look at the world through courageous eyes, believe in themselves, stretch. As I rearrange the haphazard drawers of clothes Ali left behind, the full repercussion of the moment hits me.

Yes, it is our fault.

(Autumn 2018)

Homecoming

At dawn, I awaken to the familiar crow of the rooster and the soulful call to prayer by the muezzin from a nearby mosque. Around the corner, a street vendor sets up a cart laden with oranges along the dusty road that will soon be clogged with every imaginable form of transportation — cars, rickshaws, motorcycles, buses and horse-drawn tongas.

In some ways, little has changed in Lahore, Pakistan, since I first traveled here more than 35 years ago to marry my husband in a small ceremony in the family home. In other ways, this sun-drenched city of 11 million near the border of India is vastly different, the calm of everyday life punctuated periodically by random suicide bombings.

Life, I realize more than ever, is about having the courage to take a leap of faith in the face of the unknown.

In 1982, marrying outside the faith flew in the face of tradition in this deeply Islamic country. Parents arranged marriages, usually to a cousin, and their sons rarely lived outside the family home. Apa's reaction still rings in my ears: "You are no longer my son," she responded when Zafar phoned his mother from London with the news he wanted to marry me.

I never took those words to heart, sensing her fear of the unknown: *Will I ever see him again?* Later, as a mother myself, I imagined the profound loss she felt at that moment and loved her all the more for finding the courage to open her heart and home, inviting us to be married in Lahore.

These memories wash over me as my daughter-in-law, Alaina,

bounds down the steps to the garden to be greeted with hugs, gifts and enthusiastic cries of "Welcome to the family!"

My son Qasim grinned, anticipating this moment when he would introduce the love of his life to an assortment of beloved cousins, aunts and uncles, most still living under the same roof. As a child, he competed in nightly games of cricket with his cousins, romped in the monsoon rains and listened for the melody of the ice cream truck in this walled garden during our summer visits. For him, this was a homecoming.

Sipping a cup of midmorning tea with my brother-in-law Abid, I smiled at the tender scene unfolding and realized I had blazed a trail, culminating in this joyful moment of unconditional acceptance and love.

Like Zafar and me, Qasim and Alaina were wed in two ceremonies, one Muslim, the other Catholic. My nephew Ather jokingly called the couple "overachievers" for making the 7,300-mile journey to Lahore for an add-on reception for the family.

And what a reception it proved to be: During our week-long visit in January, Alaina's parents, our traveling companions, marveled at the endless displays of hospitality and discovered what I learned a long time ago: Pakistanis may be the most gracious people on the planet. The family organized outings to a centuries-old mosque, a sleek contemporary shopping mall, an outdoor bazaar and a restored Mughal-era bathhouse. We were treated to afternoon tea and exquisite meals in restaurants and country clubs. Caught up in the patriotic fervor at the changing-of-the guard ceremony at the heavily guarded Wagah Station along the border of Pakistan and India, we chanted "Pakistan Zindabad!" (Long live Pakistan!), surrounded by hundreds of Pakistanis shrouded in the evening fog.

At the end of our stay, more than 200 family members gathered to congratulate the newlyweds over a dinner of spicy chicken, basmati rice, naan and sweet gulab jamun.

As each family posed for photos with the newlyweds, the camera's lens captured more than just the happy moment.

It captured the bond that unites us — our common humanity.

(Winter 2018)

One Heart with Courage

Dear Ali,

I wasn't wild about your idea to spend six weeks in Zambia this summer — even though I couldn't place the country on a map.

I now know this sparsely populated, impoverished land about the size of Texas is rich in culture and natural beauty. It's the home of one spectacular waterfall that most of us will only marvel at in photos. And it enjoys a reputation as one of the safest countries in Africa.

These are all reassuring facts for an anxious mother as her 18-year-old makes an 8,000-mile journey around the world to live in a wondrous, new culture.

Unlike other countries in the region, Zambia has avoided an Ebola outbreak, but it faces an HIV/AIDS epidemic. The statistics are staggering: A reported 1 in 7 adults lives with HIV, and AIDS orphans make up half of all orphans in the country. In the villages, you'll see children whose growth and brain development have been stunted by malnutrition. Families mourn the death of loved ones all too often.

This enormous health crisis in the midst of overwhelming poverty will open your eyes to a world few Americans ever experience. In the words of activist actor Martin Sheen, "Remember this above all: One heart with courage is a majority."

I admire your courage.

At your age, I boarded an airplane for the first time in my life — not to travel to a developing nation to teach youth but to visit my grandmother in Florida and enjoy a week of beach living.

Your summer will not be a walk on the beach. Once you land in Lusaka, it will take 14 hours to reach the village where you will teach — and where you will sacrifice so much of what we take for granted. Daily showers. Reliable electricity. Ridiculously expensive coffee. Tweeting. "I need a break from the First World," you said.

I admire your selflessness.

You are unlike many of your peers, who are chasing after a college degree like a carousel's brass ring. You want more in life than just a piece of parchment and the economic security it promises. You want a life with meaning.

I admire your perspective.

This spring, I introduced you to my favorite author, Anne Lamott, who writes simply and eloquently about what it means to live a life that matters. Remember her words from a commencement address at Berkeley a decade ago? She told graduates:

Every single spiritual tradition says the same three things:

1) Live in the now, as often as you can, a breath here, a moment there.

2) You reap exactly what you sow.

3) You must take care of the poor, or you are so doomed that we can't help you.

I admire your compassion.

You are ready to change the world, but this trip will change you, and you will struggle to return to the life you left.

"Once you go overseas and experience life in a different way, you are changed. And you can't really come back to the life you had," says my friend Ann Hudock, senior vice president of international programs for Plan International USA, who recently returned from living and working in Zambia. "You look at everything differently. Even little things like, 'why are there 64,000 brands of toothpaste or peanut butter' and then there are places where food doesn't get to the people who need it. It just makes no sense and is overwhelming."

Encouraged and supported by the Marianists at the University of Dayton, Ann boarded a plane for Sierra Leone after graduation. Her journey to Africa 25 years ago set her on a career path in international development that led to living in Hanoi, Vietnam, and Lusaka.

"The rural areas in Zambia with grinding poverty and dispersed population make it so hard to change things," Ann observes. "Yet there are amazing people doing just that. ... But in big ways, experiences like this can make you rethink what you want to do in life. And, that's wonderful but daunting."

In life, we're only promised the moment. Use this moment to immerse yourself in Zambia. Make new friends. Be open. Ask questions. Reflect. Read. Pray.

Above all, be yourself. You are a gift to the world.

With much love and prayers,

Mom

(Spring 2015)

God's Work

As a mother, I'm drawn to newspaper headlines about child abuse, but I tend to push the images out of my head.

The stark news about the torture and murder of street children in Guatemala and the battering of babies in Dayton, Ohio, seems worlds away from the innocent chatter of my talkative 4-year-old strapped in his car seat.

"Mommy, if I close my eyes, I can make bad guys," Ali says, holding his small fists over his eyes during a recent morning commute. "They're *real* bad guys, but their guns are pretend."

He knows there are bad people out there, but violence is not part of his world.

Too many other kids are not so fortunate. I think about the tireless work of two men who are champions for children in their backyard and around the world. Their roads crossed on campus during the University of Dayton's international conference on children's rights.

One is the father of two, the youngest jokingly described as a 9-year-old "terrorist." The other is childless but runs a major university. Both are doing what Bruce Harris describes as "God's work."

As executive director of Casa Alianza, the Latin American branch of Covenant House, Harris helps street children — homeless kids who have fallen through the cracks in countries with no social service safety nets.

As president of the University of Dayton, Brother Ray Fitz is leading the effort to redesign the child protection system in

Ohio's Montgomery County after several highly publicized deaths of children from abuse.

They share a passion for children that's compelling. Their stories move people. Their experiences have transformed their lives so much that they can't turn back — or turn their backs.

Harris refuses to part with the image of one child, branded indelibly in his mind. "He's the first child I had ever seen dead. It was the epitome of cruelty, the epitome of the waste of a human life," says Harris as he accepts the University of Dayton's Monsignor Oscar Romero Award for Leadership in Service to Human Rights.

In 1990, Nahamán Carmona Lopez, 13, was sniffing glue with four other homeless boys in a city park when he was brutally kicked and beaten by police officers in Guatemala. He died 10 days later. His gravestone reads, *I only wanted to be a child, but they wouldn't let me.*

"Kids came to us and told us who did it, that it was uniformed policemen," Harris retells a story he has told hundreds of times. "Instead of kids talking about Pokemon and Barbie dolls, they're talking about death. The world is very cruel to children. You can either throw in the towel or say, 'Who did it?' We chose the route of 'Who did it?'"

For that, he's received death threats, survived an assassination attempt and moved his family from Guatemala to Costa Rica out of fear for their safety. The four police officers were indicted.

"Children shouldn't have to suffer. If you wouldn't want it to happen to your own children, how can you let it happen to others? When the family ends, the street begins," he says.

Fitz's mind is filled with of dozens of disturbing stories he heard while co-chairing Montgomery County's Child Protection Task Force. But as with Harris, one image crowds out the others.

"Particularly painful was the story of a drug-dependent mother who wanted to become clean for the sake of her child but was not able to find an open slot in a drug-treatment program because she was poor.

"This was burned in my imagination. Why is it so difficult to protect children and support families at the same time?" he asks.

Under Fitz's leadership, the community task force spent 18 months reviewing the child protection system and made 54 recommendations for improvement. Since 1995, the county has implemented 95 percent of the suggestions and grades its efforts on an annual Valentine's Day report card. New reports of child abuse declined 15 percent in one recent year.

"We have phenomenal problems, but what I've learned has changed my life," he says. "I learned about the indomitable spirit of hope that can't be quenched. ... People daily in a heroic way are giving their lives for children."

When Fitz steps down as president, he plans to continue to work on behalf of children and families — and educate college students to do the same. "We need to create a world that gives priority to our children," he says.

It echoes an observation made by Harris: "Hopefully, one day we'll invest in kids because we care about them."

As my son imagines a safe world, two men work for a world that's safe for all children.

(Spring 2001)

Postscript: Brother Raymond L. Fitz was president of the University of Dayton for 23 years. He stepped down in 2002 and became the Ferree Professor of Social Justice.

A Warrior

You can call him the Cal Ripken of higher education.

In 26 years, Joe Belle hadn't missed a day of work.

You can call him a media darling.

He periodically shows up on the local evening news to talk about anything from the University of Dayton's plans to build new housing to disciplinary action following "some chaos" in the student neighborhood.

You can call him a warrior.

In May, Belle, who rarely took an aspirin for a headache, "went to war" and underwent a delicate six-hour operation to remove a cancerous tumor in his brain.

Just don't "make me out to be a God," said Belle, who finished a regimen of 40 radiation treatments in July and has signed up for experimental gene therapy.

On July 8, seven weeks after surgery, Belle walked out of a meeting with his neurosurgeon and into a staff meeting in UD's Kennedy Union. "The therapies are all done," he announced, then broke the stillness in the room with a self-deprecating remark about his adventures in speech therapy. "I'm tired of hearing about Dick and Jane," he quipped.

In Belle fashion, he swiftly praised his staff. "We haven't missed a beat. That's because of you."

After three decades at the University of Dayton — first as an education student in 1969, then as a resident assistant in Stuart Hall to positions with progressively more responsibilities in the student development division — the Bronx native sets a pace few can match. The first person to arrive at his Gosiger Hall office in the morning, sometimes just before the sun pokes out, he makes a pot of coffee and helpfully pulls out chairs so the house-keeper can vacuum more easily. His evenings are punctuated with meetings with students on campus or with the Brown-Warren Business Association or the Kettering Planning Commission, which he serves as vice chair. If there's a fire in a campus house or a disturbance on a campus street, he often fields the typically late-night calls.

Some say the 5-foot-5-inch Belle, a second-generation Italian-American with a quick stride and an infectious smile, rules the student neighborhood much like a village mayor.

Belle is tackling his brain tumor with the same take-charge attitude he uses when negotiating prices for house purchases or helping students open their own convenience store or talking to reporters about plans to prevent out-of-control parties on St. Patrick's Day.

He's upbeat. He's optimistic. He's realistic.

Currently, there's no cure for the type of tumor — a grade four glioblastoma multiforme — that stole into his head this spring with a pounding headache.

"If they (the doctors) have to tinker, you'd rather it be some-where else than in your head," he says quietly. "We're taking the most aggressive approach in battling this type of cancer. I tell the doctors, 'You do your part, and I'll do my part.' I'm holding onto my endurance and keeping my body strong."

Belle has received so many supportive phone calls and notes that his wife, Barb, worked with UD's "techno priest," Father Jerry Chinchar in campus ministry, to create a website that chronicles Belle's progress and celebrates such milestones as the end of radiation treatments and the finale of a short-lived beard.

In mid-July, his doctors gave him the go-ahead to come in the office one day a week, but he's also conducting a lot of work from home.

"I'm a doer," he said. "I can't be productive if I'm sitting at home. It's that Italian upbringing. You get to church and you get to school. One of my sons once asked me, 'Why are you always in the office so early, Dad? Aren't you the boss?'

"Well, the boss leads."

(Autumn 1999)

On the Other Side of Fear

"You don't have to be 21 to have your whole life ahead of you."

With those simple words, author and actress Kathy Kinney uncovered one of the secrets behind the enormous popularity of the University of Dayton's Erma Bombeck Writers' Workshop.

It's empowering.

The 2016 workshop sold out in five hours and 41 minutes, with writers making the creative pilgrimage to campus from all parts of the United States, Canada and Spain. Thanks to the ongoing generosity of the Alumni Association, nearly 20 communication students soaked in the inspiration and writing tips, too, from an all-star roster that featured humorist Roy Blount Jr., novelist Amy Ephron, *Saturday Night Live* writer Alan Zweibel and *New York Times* bestselling author Jenny Lawson.

Writers know this biennial workshop, launched in 2000, is not like any other in the country. I've described it as part love letter, part family reunion, part pep talk. Kinney and her writing partner Cindy Ratzlaff brought the encouragement writers need to face a blank page or forge through a horrible first draft.

"Everything you want is on the other side of fear," said Kinney, perhaps best known for her portrayal of the campy Mimi on *The Drew Carey Show*. "Just walk through it."

Every time I enter the packed Dayton Marriott Hotel ballroom for the opening keynote dinner, I'm taken aback by the energy and exuberance, by the laughter and warmth. As the 20th anniversary of Erma's death approached this spring, I felt her legacy even more deeply through a new generation of writers who gathered in her memory to laugh, learn and support one another on the often-lonely writing journey.

"We cannot think of a better legacy for our mom than this workshop," Matt Bombeck said midway through the event as he introduced a new one-woman show, *Erma Bombeck: At Wit's End*, that sparked tears and laughter.

In Bombeck's heyday, her column appeared in 900 newspapers. She wrote 12 books, nine of which appeared on *The New York Times* bestsellers list. For 11 years, Americans woke up to her humorous segments on *Good Morning America*. A 1949 University of Dayton alumna, she never forgot "three magic words" from Brother Tom Price, her English professor. After she slipped a humorous essay under his door, he greeted her with words that sustained her the rest of her life: "You can write!"

That's the spirit we try to bottle in an event that has, largely by word of mouth, gained national prominence and a loyal following of writers who affectionately call themselves a tribe.

"What happens when 350 people, predominantly women, truck in from all across the U.S. to spend three full days laughing (and a little crying), eating (mostly desserts) and baring their souls to each other? Magic. In a place called Dayton. That's not a punchline," blogged Kimberly "Kimba" J. Dalferes, a former Justice Department official-turned-book author.

Creativity coach Julia Roberts called the workshop "a utopia for humor writers that only appears every other year, out of the mist, on the edge of the Great Miami River in Dayton, Ohio (like *Brigadoon*)."

For me, the workshop's power can be found in the small moments: At lunch one day, emcee Pat Wynn Brown surprised long-retired schoolteacher Lori Mansell by "crowning" her queen. Refusing to take her tiara off, Mansell enjoyed the curtsies and bows from other attendees all afternoon — then went home to Carmel, Indiana, and wrote and published her first essay.

"It's never too late to start writing," Brown said, noting that Mansell already had a knack for defying age: She once told her tap dance group she was only 76 "because they kick you out at 80."

It's a lesson worth living — and one that our conference attendees take to heart: You don't have to be 21 to have your whole life ahead of you.

(Spring 2016)

Diana

For one crazy moment, in the midst of all the delirium around Princess Diana's death, Cynthia Fodor almost convinced me to jump on a plane to London.

After being out of touch for more than a decade, we had decided, in the span of a five-minute telephone conversation, to write the definitive book on Diana, Princess of Wales. After all, we had both worked for ABC News in London during the 1981 Royal Wedding hoopla.

Cynthia had spent more than six months preparing fat briefing books full of facts to feed to anchors Peter Jennings and Barbara Walters during ABC's live coverage of the event from a balcony on St. Paul's Cathedral. Now an anchorwoman herself, she still has boxes of index cards brimming with notes from interviews with Diana's childhood friends and interesting tidbits about her gleaned from London's colorful, if not always accurate, press.

I have nothing other than some memories and a laminated ABC press badge with a wedding logo. When ABC News asked Cynthia to work as a full-time researcher for its Royal Wedding coverage, I got her job as the bureau's general-assignment researcher simply because I was in the right place at the right time. Cynthia learned about everything royal, while I devoured a daily diet of London newspapers — from the staid *Times* to the cheeky *Sun* with its Page 3 pinup girl — in the quest to build a file of upcoming stories that might appeal to an American audience.

When producers called from *Frightline* — what we jokingly dubbed *Nightline* because it required us to arrange interviews with members of Parliament in the middle of the night — I received the joyous duty of asking people to skip sleep to be on American TV. For a journalist fresh out of college, those were unforgettable times.

And there was nothing more memorable than the Royal Wedding. As I stood in ABC's London bureau and watched the pageantry unfold on live television, I couldn't help but feel a part of history — even though I would go back to a Bayswater flat that night and joke with my British roommates about the monarchy being somewhat like Oz.

A Pakistani — the man who was to eventually become my husband — skipped work that day and made his way through the crowd to catch a glimpse of the royal procession. More than 16 years later, we would lie in bed just before dawn and listen to Elton John sorrowfully sing of a candle burned out in the wind. Right or wrong, few people from our generation have captured the worldwide imagination quite like England's "golden child."

On the surface, the former kindergarten teacher who married a prince appeared to live a fairy tale. Instead, she spent her youth trapped in a loveless marriage in the class-conscious British monarchy where people maintain a stiff upper lip and do what's expected of them. Like millions of others around the world, I became drawn to her when she quit doing what was expected. She was painfully human and candidly admitted her insecurities, including an eating disorder. Unlike other members of the Royal Family, she openly showed compassion for strangers and hugged her sons in public. Her greatest gift, her brother told us, was her intuition.

I was only a few years older than Diana when I spontaneously threw clothes in a suitcase and returned to London, without a job or a place to live, to figure out whether a two-week romance at the end of a three-month internship with McGraw-Hill World

News in London was true love. I don't know whether I would have acted so impetuously if I had known that my husband's Muslim family was already in the midst of arranging a marriage for him. Much like Prince Charles, he found himself between his heart and his head, between duty and a departure from tradition. He followed his heart — yet never forgot his roots.

Could this tragedy have been prevented if Prince Charles had entered into marriage for the right reason, if he had remained true to himself? "If he had just married Camilla (Parker Bowles, his old flame), he could have saved everyone this aggravation," said Cynthia, my former ABC News colleague, echoing what many mused in the days following Diana's death.

Unfortunately, Prince Charles didn't follow his heart. Diana nearly always did. In hindsight, it's not difficult to predict the tragedy of those two lives.

Indeed, it has all the makings of a great book.

(Winter 1997)

'Never Again,' Again

Richard Holbrooke commands attention. He even overshadows a former prime minister in the room.

It's hard not to pay attention to a man credited with ending a war that claimed the lives of 300,000 people in the former Yugoslavia, a man sent to the region to negotiate a truce in Kosovo, a man whose gift of negotiation and unflappable diplomacy have made him larger than life in the eyes of the international community.

On the eve of the third anniversary of the Dayton Peace Accords, the University of Dayton honored the diplomat with an honorary degree in recognition of his "relentless, principled and imaginative pursuit of lasting peace as something better than the final epigraph of the battlefield."

In his shadow during the ceremony stood a man who told the world about a catastrophic genocide in his country and quietly reminded us that it can happen again, that history does repeat itself for those not paying attention.

"We said 'never again' some 50 years ago," Haris Silajdzic said softly, "and then Bosnia happened in global peacetime and broke this last barrier of hope. After Bosnia, everything is possible if we do not do it right."

Silajdzic had returned to Dayton, Ohio, the site of 21 days of often-testy negotiations, to honor Holbrooke, an envoy "who never crossed the line of evil," he noted. "He was always on the side of good" during the complex, sometimes theatrical mediation that Holbrooke recounts in his memoir, *To End a War*.

Silajdzic nominated the veteran diplomat for the Nobel Peace Prize for his efforts to bring peace to the troubled region.

Yet it was Silajdzic who first drew international attention to massacres in towns and villages in Bosnia and Herzegovina and negotiated with governments to allow almost 2 million refugees to find asylum outside the borders of his homeland, which had turned into a killing field. Silajdzic, a philosopher by training, remains passionately committed to human rights — especially bringing at-large war criminals to justice — and wants to believe that people can live in peaceful coexistence in a multiethnic society.

"Bosnia is probably the most pluralistic country in the world. We have the most pluralistic, multicultural, multiethnic, multireligious society. We showed the way. We were the successful monument. We still are the paradigm of the future. Bosnia reflects not only the state of mind, but the state of heart, of humanity," he said.

Compelling words. Still, Silajdzic wonders if the world has learned any lessons from Bosnia. He worries about those who have lost their souls.

"We have to take care of our souls, take care of the fact that no civilization can survive without the minimum of morality," he said. Then, with a caution: "Beware of empty hearts. They're much more dangerous than empty pockets. In my country, we were not killed by people hungry for bread, but hungry for (a) soul.

"Generations of young men and women were taught to hate. We're still a rich country, but we lack — and those who did it to us lack — soul," he said. "It was a plan, not just of genocide. ... People wanted to erase memories; people wanted to kill people, to ethnically cleanse them forever. If we could get through the Middle Ages, through the First World War, through the Second World War and keep the monuments of four cultures in my country, then how come it all came to an end at the end of the 20th century with a big crash?"

He reminded those of us who have never fled our country because of fear or been dismissed from a job because of our faith that "large and blatant en masse violations of human rights still flourish."

He called for "enough sense and enough moral fortitude" to pursue the implementation of human rights in the region.

Expressing cautious optimism, he said, "We can put this Dayton agreement in the last page in the book of humanity of the 20th century. It was a successful century but also one that killed 180 million people in two wars and showed the worst face of humanity. I would like to put it in the first page of the new book of humanity in a century in which things will have a price but not (at all costs), so (we) have some values, too."

He spoke the words quietly, their meaning hanging in the air. For a moment, the spotlight shifted from Holbrooke.

Are we paying attention?

(Winter 1998)

An Irish Wedding in the Countryside

It is not a particularly uncommon sight during an Irish Catholic wedding: A member of the bride's family offers a hand across the church aisle to a member of the groom's family in a "sign of peace."

The vignette, lasting only a few seconds, leaves a far-lasting impression on an American visitor. The man who extends his hand so willingly hails from the Catholic section of strife-torn Belfast in British-ruled Northern Ireland. The recipient, a Yorkshire native, has traveled across the Irish Sea to witness a marriage between a Catholic and a Protestant, an Irish woman and an English man.

Set in the tiny fishing village of Greystones, 18 miles south of Dublin in the semi-neutral territory of the Irish Republic, the London couple's wedding transpires with no more than the usual pre-ceremony jitters. Only a few wedding guests mention "the troubles," as the Irish label the bloody tapestry of sectarian violence responsible for the loss of more than 2,000 lives since 1969, and they are curious Americans who cannot leave well enough alone.

"Belfast is a dump," says Stephen of his bride May's hometown on an outing to Dublin a day before the wedding. "People have gotten married there and gotten shot outside the church. You go into a pub on the Falls Road (in the city's Catholic district), and the men will be sitting with their heads hunched over a table planning to blow up something," says the red-haired Yorkshire youth. "They travel in pairs to the toilet. It puts me on edge."

The bride, whose family has steadfastly refused to move off the battered Falls Road, used to bring rubber bullets back to her

London roommates as souvenirs. May scoffed at the 1981 racial riots in England's capital city, calling them boring compared to the "excitement in the air" around Belfast when the night is abruptly illuminated by petrol bombs and shattered by the wailing of police sirens. But even she nixed chancing a wedding in the North where violence can erupt like a summer cloudburst seemingly out of nowhere.

"It's a dump," May agrees, "and you might get blown up."

Particularly if you speak in a crisp British accent rather than a telltale American drawl that every non-American who's ever watched *Starsky & Hutch* can immediately identify.

"I wouldn't have come if the wedding had been in Belfast," a Brit who sells tickets on London's subway system says flatly between bites of roast beef at the lavish reception dinner. "With my British accent, I'd be nervous. I'd be afraid if I went to buy a newspaper, the word would get out, 'There's a Brit in town. Who is he? Is he part of the Army? Is he part of the intelligence service?'"

In Greystones, nobody cares if a Brit pops in. A hand-scrawled poetic Gaelic verse greets wedding guests at the seaside La Touche Hotel: *Cead mile failte*, "a hundred thousand welcomes!" Time stands still here. Stray dogs meander along the village's narrow streets, occasionally plopping down in front of O'Brien's off-license liquor store or one of several butcher shops to watch the day's assorted traffic. Teenage girls in traditional Catholic school skirts amble toward the bakery as a few tourists head toward the unpopulated beach for a stroll along the Irish Sea. A young mother leisurely pushes a pram down the sidewalk, her two fair-haired sons zipped in raincoat ponchos up to their necks in the event of a midmorning drizzle. A topaz-shelled snail inches slowly up a stone wall that surrounds a spacious bungalow like a well-trimmed hedge.

Nobody's in a mad rush. A snail's pace is appropriate in the untroubled seaside resort that sits in the heart of County Wicklow, known as "the garden of Ireland."

We find ourselves in this lush green Irish village via a self-proposed itinerary few travel agents would recommend to more well-heeled tourists. We fly from Salt Lake City to Newark, where we bravely board People Express Airlines' brand-new $298 round-trip, no-frills transatlantic flight to London. After a few days touring there, we hop on a British Rail train for a five-hour traverse of English and Welsh countryside. The train rolls to a stop in the coastal town of Holyhead in North Wales, where we catch the sea-link ferry for a three-and-a-half-hour journey across the surprisingly placid Irish Sea.

A white-haired, Dublin born-and-bred taxi driver meets us at the Dún Laoghaire pier. A free spirit, he calmly sails through red lights. "The traffic lights never work in Ireland," he says brightly, giving us our first brush with Irish humor and an indication we would not be staying in a particularly large resort town. "You'll have to put me up for bed and breakfast at the hotel," he quips in a soft, lilting brogue. "I'll never get a fare back from Greystones. The days of miracles are gone."

That's the quiet charm of this picturesque village on the southeast coast of Ireland. For those desiring a taste of urban life, the congested sidewalks of Dublin are a short bus ride away. A modern city that retains an 18th-century atmosphere through its Georgian squares, such as Merrion Square where Oscar Wilde and W.B. Yeats once lived, Dublin also boasts a spectrum of specialty shops offering cut glass, tweeds, jewelry, Aran knitwear, Belleek china and linens.

"Greystones is a wee bit of Cornwall in Ireland," says May, reminding me of our adventure-filled hitchhiking escapade one weekend when we shared a flat in London together. As we stroll to her brother Patrick's house for an evening tea of sausages, soda bread and strong, hot tea mellowed with a generous helping of cream, she informs us matter-of-factly that the family "shipped" Patrick to southern Ireland several years ago to ensure his safety.

This is her only allusion to "the troubles," which seem light years away instead of 100 miles north to the heavily patrolled border. There are more pressing matters to worry about: Who's to make the garter forgotten in the rush of last-minute wedding preparations? Will anyone in the wedding party trip over the video camera wires (bound to look out of place in Holy Rosary Church, a staid, aged granite monument to Catholicism)? Will it rain, drizzle or downpour on the wedding morn?

Notably absent are reputed Irish superstitions — worries about meeting a funeral on the way to church or hopes of hearing three magpies on the wedding morning as a promise of good luck. Still, Stephen and May vow to avoid each other the entire day before the wedding as a token nod to tradition. As luck will have it, however, they accidentally run into each other in the pouring rain outside Barnaby, the whitewashed pub in the village's center. Stephen cannot be more delighted and insists any chance meeting is indeed good luck.

Fortune does shine on the couple. A dreary overcast morning metamorphoses only minutes before the ceremony into a cheery, sunny afternoon.

"I said to our Kathleen, 'Isn't that a bit of blue behind all that gray?'" says May, who earlier predicted "buckets of rain" for the ceremony. "It was a miracle how the sky cleared. I was immediately converted back to the Catholic faith."

Like most weddings, months of worry boil down to a quick ceremony that's over with a sigh of relief before you realize it.

The couple exchange traditional vows full of tongue-twisting "thees" and "thous." Sounds of the awe-inspiring "Ave Maria" and "Amazing Grace" fill the church.

The guests walk a few steps back to the La Touche Hotel for a reception of rich food and bubbly champagne and an evening of toastmaking, singing and dancing. Between the all-too-familiar strains of Frank Sinatra's "New York, New York" and John Denver's "Annie's Song," the band lunges into sprightly Irish jigs and invites guests to take the microphone. Stephen's grandfather sings a peppy Yorkshire tune in a deep, resonant voice. May's mother, with all the poise of a street troubadour, serenades the crowd with a bittersweet Irish folk song, "A Bunch of Thyme."

Come all ye maidens young and fair
All you that are blooming in your prime
Always beware and keep your garden fair
Let no man steal away your thyme
For thyme, it is a precious thing
And thyme brings all things to my mind
Thyme with all its flavor along with all its joy
Thyme brings all things to my mind
Once she had a bunch of thyme
She thought it would never decay
Then came a lusty sailor
Who chanced to pass her way
He stole her bunch of thyme away
The sailor gave her a rose
A rose that never would decay
He gave it to her to keep her reminded
Of when he stole her thyme away
So come all ye maidens young and fair

All you that are blooming in your prime
Always beware and keep your garden fair
Let no man steal away your thyme
For thyme, it is a precious thing
And thyme brings all things to my mind
Thyme with all its flavor along with all its joy
Thyme brings all things to an end

The ballad's sad, haunting melody lingers long after the music has faded. But "a bit of blue" shows through — like the firm handshake between a Catholic and a Protestant. Like the love between two soulmates courageous enough to marry in the middle of "the troubles."

This moment, it seems, marks a beginning, not an end. That's a meaningful message to take home.

(Autumn 1983)

SWAT Team of Love

"You must write about your mailbox," Pat insisted over lunch on Lindey's leafy courtyard patio.

It had been more than a year since we had last gathered to eat, laugh and solve every problem known to woman. Today's lunch felt like a gift. The potted begonias bloomed with exuberance, and the gentle springtime breeze held a promise of more carefree days ahead. Filled with the hope of putting COVID-19 in the rearview mirror, I was looking ahead, not behind me.

But then Pat reminded me that not every awful moment in life deserves to be repressed or discarded like a painful childhood memory.

Before my husband retrieved the newspaper one March morning two years earlier, an explosive device detonated in our mailbox, which sits down a long driveway on a quiet country road. It warped the sturdy steel slot and shattered our last smidgen of innocence about the kind of country we have become.

In another era, I would have dismissed this incident as a prank, but none of our neighbors' mailboxes was targeted: only ours, and we don't hide who we are. An American citizen for decades, my husband openly talks about his Muslim faith and Pakistani heritage to anyone who asks, whether it's curious friends at backyard graduation cookouts or those who stop by our annual Christmas party, the only one in our neighborhood with spicy chicken tikka masala and samosas on the buffet island.

After 9/11, I feared for my family's safety, but the greatest crisis in life is one of imagination. Two decades later, hatred for "the other" has been mainstreamed, a legacy of the man who once served as the most powerful leader in the world. No other president in history had attacked immigrants and people of color as Donald Trump did. Is it any wonder hate crimes spiked during his presidency?

Just four days before someone blew up our mailbox, a white supremacist, who described Trump as "a symbol of renewed white identity," opened fire in two mosques in Christchurch, New Zealand, and killed 51 people during Friday prayers. He livestreamed the mass murders on Facebook.

Against this backdrop, our police chief, Dayton's bomb squad and the FBI weren't taking any chances, and neither were we. Law enforcement officers characterized our mailbox incident as a possible hate crime, and we immediately put our neighbors on high alert, hired a private guard and installed security cameras.

I urged the family to keep a low profile, but our son, Ali, begged us not to keep quiet. In his description of the pre-dawn explosion on Instagram, he included a photo of our two-religion, two-culture family at his brother's joyful wedding reception in Lahore, Pakistan.

"Thankfully, we are safe," he wrote. "Please understand that this is not normal. This is not okay. But, unfortunately, this is not surprising. My family has always been outspoken — advocating with unwavering dedication for racial, religious and educational justice in a town and country that are not always kind to those seeking justice. We are not scared. Our voices will not be silenced. We will always embrace peace, love and kindness. Love will always outweigh hate. This dark chapter in American history will not define our lives."

We were deluged with love and support from family, friends, neighbors, community leaders — even people we barely knew.

"I love you, brother," wrote one of Ali's high school friends. "This is horrible," echoed others. And the common refrain: "I stand with you."

When I shared my fear about retribution, my friends formed a battalion.

"Darling, keep me on your SWAT team of love," emailed Pat. "I am from the west side of Columbus. I have fought repeatedly. I know I look like I am a weak cheerleader showgirl, but guess what? I could guard your house. And I would do it."

I'll always remember the unexpected gestures of kindness and empathy. Ellie, a University of Dayton student I met once, shared how she and a friend ventured outside their comfort zone during spring break and joined Muslims gathering for Friday prayers at a London mosque.

"This house of God was a place of welcome to me," she wrote. "It was a simple time, a break from the bustling city and a beautiful encounter with new communities."

Later that same evening, she was horrified to learn about the New Zealand massacre of Muslims. "Fear, desolation and despair are the agenda of these attackers and of evil. … We must join as a community to fight them. Our greatest offense is to be filled with a radical hope and love. And I cannot imagine or comprehend the turmoil in your family's hearts right now, but I pray you find rest in knowing that you are surrounded by communities that love you, that hope for better and that will stand next to you always."

I wiped away tears, realizing that with a SWAT team of love behind us, hate never had a fighting chance.

(Summer 2021)

FRIENDSHIP

As the Screens Come Up, the Walls Come Down

Afflicted with cabin fever about a month into the pandemic, I tapped out a note to my journalism friends from Ohio University, where decades ago we chased stories and dreams.

"If your Zoom dance card isn't full, a few of us thought it might be fun to reconnect over drinks and the miles at 5 p.m. on Saturday," I wrote.

Seconds later, Scott quipped, "Sounds great! I'll pick up the check."

"Can't wait to see all your tiny smiling faces," responded Dee Dee, signaling the beginning of regular Zoom dates, the rectangles multiplying as old friends join the periodic video calls.

I never thought it possible to be cloistered and connected, yet, to my surprise, my relationships today are more intentional and emotionally intimate than ever — and I haven't stepped foot in a coffee shop to meet a friend in 10 months and counting.

Every night, shortly after 5 p.m., my social worker son calls from New York City to chat about his work counseling HIV-positive adults, the latest adventures with Link (his roommate's deaf rescue dog) and that night's vegan recipe. My phone, markedly quieter before the pandemic, now dings daily with text messages from my college roommates, my older son or friends from across town, on the other side of our rural road or on the opposite coast.

"Can't sleep! So excited for a new beginning," a neighbor interrupted my sleep with a 5:30 a.m. text on Inauguration Day.

"Hot Pockets recalled. That's IT. That's my bad-news tipping point. I'm out," texted a close friend from LA in one of her hilarious messages.

And every few weeks, my j-school friends gather to check in on each other, analyze the day's headlines and renew friendships that began over all-nighters pulled together producing a daily student newspaper in a small Appalachian college town. Scattered now from Manhattan to Seattle, these are some of the most fascinating people I know—curious, inquisitive, compassionate and unfailing in truth-telling. They are the storytellers who will chronicle the unfamiliar road we're traversing for the pages of history.

Stories — as personal as a coronavirus diagnosis or as chilling as an insurrection at the Capitol — bring us together like hummingbirds to nectar. But it's friendship cultivated over 40 years that keeps us moored.

"We know each other the way children who grow up together know each other," said Anne, a health reporter.

Still held largely captive in our homes, we talk about our lives in isolation and playfully tease each other. "None of those classes helped you, Larry, because you didn't go to them," Peggy, a contact tracer, told an AP reporter to laughter. "We've come full circle," I told Theresa, a space reporter at *Breaking Defense* who was carded when she showed up early for "senior shopping" at her neighborhood grocery store.

During our college days writing and editing for *The Post*, we stood on the cusp of careers that would bring us into the lives of readers. These days we find ourselves peering into each other's lives. After her son suddenly lost his job, a friend fought back tears and shared her worry about his future. As writers who respect facts, we're dismayed by those in our own families who embrace unfounded conspiracy theories. Choking back disappointment, we cancel Christmas plans with relatives after a new surge in the virus.

During these socially distant times, we show up for each other — and show vulnerability. We've learned to be gentle with ourselves. Every video call now ends with two words, "Love you!"

Turning wistful as the conversation wound down one week, Larry quietly urged us to live life without hesitation. "The road behind us is longer than the road ahead. Embrace every moment. Find that moment of joy."

As I clicked "leave meeting" on the laptop screen, I realized the pandemic would end eventually, but friendship might be the one immunity that lasts a lifetime.

(Winter 2021)

Lessons in Living

"It's just about the moments. That's all life really is," my friend Jim said quietly over the phone after breaking the news that he had been diagnosed with inoperable lung cancer.

I have known no one better than Jim at living in the moment. Most of us are too busy choreographing the future.

I flashed back to 1979 as Jim and my college roommates, Toni and Denise, belted out — complete with synchronized hand gestures — "Stop in the Name of Love" in our living room.

After graduation, Denise's camera captured us outside a London tube station, surrounded by a mountain of luggage and an avalanche of apprehension. This was the start of a post-college adventure decided on impulse late one night at the kitchen table. As the only one who had stepped foot in England before, Jim helped orient us before heading to Amsterdam for an internship with the Associated Press while I stayed to work for McGraw-Hill World News.

After returning home, we surprised our parents with the news that we were flying back across the Atlantic again — without jobs this time. We had talked each other into taking a chance on newfound loves. I eventually married mine.

When Jim told me he was dying, I yearned to sit down at the computer keyboard to tease from my heart all the right words. Instead, I bought an airline ticket to New York City.

We sorted through faded issues of the *Butler Aviator*, the high school newspaper we edited, and fondly recalled our principal, who excused us from some classes after we told him we took home "midnight oil pages" to proof. While our peers were stuck in civics, we ran to the printer and skipped cafeteria food for tastier lunches and long conversations at a tiny café in a nearby town. Was it ink in the blood or the joy of newfound freedom that drew us to journalism?

For me, that call may have gone unanswered without Jim's insistence that I transfer from community college to journalism school. I enrolled at Ohio University, sight unseen, with few funds or much faith in myself.

A gifted writer, Jim was named editor of *The Post*, the daily student newspaper, and assigned me the managing editor's role. We spent our days chasing stories and our nights singing along to Frankie Valli and the Four Seasons and Slim Whitman tunes in those slap-happy predawn hours spent putting the paper to bed.

More than 26 years later, as Jim lies on the couch tethered to oxygen, we eat bagels, chat about everything and nothing, and listen to Lesley Gore croon "You Don't Own Me" and "It's My Party (I'll Cry If I Want To)." There were no tears, only the words you speak when you worry you won't get another chance.

I thanked him for helping me believe in myself at a vulnerable time in my life, for writing the treasured box of letters stored in the attic, for sharing homespun short stories for my editing eye — and for amusing me with the way he saw the world.

It's not often a friend uses "exquisite, sultry and sublime" all in the same sentence, but that's how he mourned his musical icon Peggy Lee in one of his more unforgettable emails.

Later that evening — his last at home before entering hospice — his close friends Jim and Dan come over, and we laugh and reminisce about music and literature and travels. At one point, despite his growing weakness, Jim bursts into a refrain from a Peggy Lee song.

As we listen in amazement, I understand with full force the lesson he taught me: "It's just about the moments."

(Summer 2006)

Going the Distance

The morning dew clings to blades of grass on my mother's grave with the same tenacity and grace she displayed during a decade of illness.

I close my eyes in prayer and memory — and imagination.

In my mind, a mockingbird flits between my mother's and grandparents' headstones at Calvary Cemetery. The words from a 95-year-old woman's letter echo in my head, chasing away the pain: "I know the very spot where your loved ones are buried. In good weather, I went with Rosalie every Sunday to water the flowers. Many Sundays a mockingbird seemed to greet us. I would follow him from statue to statue, almost like playing tag. Rosalie wasn't quite as fleet of foot, but would laugh and laugh."

For more than a dozen years, my grandmother Rosalie Krimm's best friend, Viola King, has scribbled long, chatty letters filled with memories of their lifelong friendship. Even after my grandmother died in 1998, the letters continued to pop up in my mailbox, a hidden treat among the bills and credit card solicitations.

Few people write real letters anymore. We send hurried emails and abbreviated text messages or make quick cell phone calls. Yet, there's something enduring and exquisite about letters written between friends.

On that cool, peaceful summer morning standing before my mother's grave, I realized how much I learned about family and friendship from those letters. They have served almost as modern-day parables helping me deal with life's twists.

A few days before Christmas in 1998, my grandmother lay

half-comatose, tethered to oxygen and holding onto a wisp of life. I read a letter to her through eyes blurred with tears. "Not a day passes that I do not pray for her and feel grief, but when the final time comes, I know I will be devastated," Viola wrote. "Can anyone realize it has been a friendship over 80 years? I was in the first grade, and she was in Miss Straley's second grade. We laughed, played, whispered, slept next to each other, sat next to each other in the dining room and got punished for the same things."

Viola's letters vividly described their growing-up years at the former Ohio Soldiers' and Sailors' Orphans' Home, their husbands, their vacations, their shared jokes. I learned about taking care of hummingbirds, canning tomatoes, concocting gourmet meals, enduring the banes of old age — even whether John Jakes' latest novel was worth the paper it was printed on.

Most of all, I learned how to nurture friendship, the kind that lasts a lifetime. Many letters ended with Viola's signature statement, "I promise to keep boring you."

When I reflect on the friendship these two women cultivated, I think of the kind of love described in 1 Corinthians: "(Love) always protects, always trusts, always hopes, always perseveres."

It's a lesson some of us keep relearning. Genuine love is not fleeting. It goes the distance, turning its back on anger, envy, pride and selfishness. That's the kind of marathon these women ran in tandem.

"I'm an observer of people," Viola wrote to me in February 2000. "I see so few with longstanding or solid friendships. I'd like to make them realize that one must be a friend in order to have friends. I feel sorry that there seems to be no depth in people's feelings. Everything seems on the surface. ... Whatever happened to the time when a cup of tea and an hour or so with a dear friend or a good neighbor were important?"

I recently made the two-hour drive to Fredericktown, Ohio, for cucumber gazpacho, a cup of tea and an afternoon of nonstop conversation with this delightful woman who's nearly twice as old as I am, with the wisdom to prove it. She regaled me with new anecdotes of childhood adventures in the orphanage, observations about our troubled world and an insider's view of life in this small-town neighborhood where her doctor makes house calls. Still nimble, she lamented how macular degeneration has robbed her of the pleasure of reading and makes writing difficult because she can see only three letters at a time. It hasn't stopped her from picking up a pen anyway.

She opened up her wallet and showed me a picture of my grandmother. "I think it would make her happy to know that I still carry this," she said.

I blinked away tears, filled with gratitude for the enduring power of their friendship. After months of quiet grief, I felt restored again.

When I step foot in the cemetery, I will listen for the song of that long-ago mockingbird — and its poignant reminder that love perseveres.

(Autumn 2007)

Glory Days

A hand-scrawled sign on a winding country road beckoned us: "Day lilies, $5."

We turned the car around and ventured into a backyard oasis of 3,500 brightly colored flowers that bloom year after year. As a friend and I picked out flowers for gardens that sit 400 miles apart, I thought about how much a perennial garden and childhood friends have in common.

Every five years, we gather together to embellish the same stories, cultivating friendships sown more than three decades ago when we were children on the school playground.

This is not a high school reunion. It's not a gathering of college roommates.

"This is remnants of your old glory days in eighth grade," teased 16-year-old Noah Krzan during a feisty late-night euchre game between my friends and their teenagers.

By the time we reached eighth grade at St. Christopher School in Vandalia, Ohio, we were 13 strong — nine girls and four boys. As Noah's father, Mike, remembered with fondness, we had "trustful fear" of our teachers, mostly nuns and priests, who taught us math, religion — and lessons about ourselves.

Nine of the original group from five states reunited one muggy June afternoon for a smorgasbord of hamburgers, beer and storytelling.

Gregg Finnegan, who runs a refrigeration and air-conditioning business in Vandalia, described the group as "sort of like a long-lost family." Our camaraderie had grown as comfortable as a pair of tennis shoes you continue to wear while newer ones sit in the closet.

"It seemed like I had seen everyone in the past few months when in some cases it's been 20 years," said Matt Stoermer, a Dayton real estate developer. "I especially liked the stories being retold, everyone chiming in with different details and perspectives. And the four of us guys throwing the baseball around like it was May of 1972. Pretty cool. All in all, (it was) a special time in our lives that we have managed to hang onto — a pretty unique situation that we shouldn't take for granted."

Now in our 40s, we don't take much for granted anymore. When we talk about our lives, it's as if we've cribbed from each other's notebooks. Under the false bravado of youth, we once acted invincible. Now we know there are no lifetime guarantees. When each day is unpredictable, you finally learn to live on life's terms.

In a year's time, one classmate watched two of her sons die of cystic fibrosis, while another lost a brother in a backpacking accident in Alaska. Another younger brother is battling a rare cancer. A teenage nephew is dying of a brain tumor. The phrase "running around" has taken on new meaning as a few have learned what it's like to sprint between a parent's hospital bed and a child's soccer game. The terrorist attacks of Sept. 11 have shaken all of us.

In times that test the soul, we find ourselves seeking out long-ago friends. We don't see each other every week, but we've not outgrown the comfort of friendship.

"This is just what I need — old friends and good conversation," said Kim Lazarevic, an emergency room nurse supervisor in a children's hospital outside Milwaukee. "I will always travel to see the old gang. We are so fortunate to have known each other. When we get together, it is like the time just melts away and we are back on the playground."

A few lingered through Sunday to attend Mass and stroll through the familiar halls of our old school, remembering the teachers who challenged and nurtured us, the baseball and spelling bee contests that gave us the confidence to risk failing.

I stopped to read a plaque that hangs in the modern addition to the school: "Their journey will take them beyond books and lead them into life."

Next spring a purple day lily will bob its head in Kim's garden, while a bright yellow one sprouts in mine.

And in five years, we'll find ourselves together again.

(Summer 2002)

Connectedness Beyond Compare

Who jumps on a plane or makes an eight-hour road trip to relive moments from grade school?

"When I told people at work I was going to my eighth-grade reunion, they looked at me like I was crazy," said Steve Stormer, a baker who flew to Dayton from a tiny town in Oklahoma to drink beer and reminisce with the other dozen who made up our class at St. Christopher School in 1972.

It had been 25 years since four boys and nine girls (three named a variation of Teresa, the ever-popular saint in the late 1950s) "graduated" from eighth grade at the Vandalia, Ohio, parochial school. On a muggy Sunday afternoon in late June we gathered at my home to take a long look at our lives since our childhood days — and our last reunion five years ago.

Some of us had gained a few pounds; others had lost some hair; and increasingly, we found ourselves part of the so-called "sandwich generation," caring for our children and, at times, our aging parents.

As the rain clouds rolled in, the memories rolled out. The women laughed at our shared recollection of testing the principal's patience by rolling up the waistbands of our uniform skirts in a spirit of rebellion. In that same spirit of growing up, we had tested the waters in a lot of areas — from a tentative first kiss on the playground to unbridled competitiveness on the softball diamond to the staging of *Jesus Christ Superstar* over the protests of Father Edwin Aufderheide, who taught us religion.

We respected our teachers but thought they were ancient. We were astonished to suddenly realize our principal, Sister Lou Ann Roof, whom we all feared at the time, was just 35 when she ruled over St. Christopher School. "That's younger than us now!" exclaimed Terri Neff, a former elementary school teacher raising three sons in a Cleveland suburb. "Please, nobody tell her I said that."

My 6-year-old scampered off to play with Luke, my childhood best friend's son. In a few hours, they became fast friends.

Mickey Dickman looked at me with a smile, "Looks familiar, doesn't it? We've come full circle."

As I gazed around at my childhood friends, I wanted to freeze the moment in my mind like a snapshot. I recalled what Kim Lazarevic, an emergency-room nurse, uttered five years ago when we huddled in lawn chairs at my house on an unseasonably cold June day. "These are some of my best friends," she said simply, as though no other explanation were needed about why she would travel all the way from Wisconsin to eat a hamburger off the grill.

It could have been a scene from *The Big Chill*, my favorite feel-good movie about the enduring power of friendship. Friendships rooted early sustain us, and no material possession comes close to the richness of feeling that connectedness with others.

A few moments in our lives hang suspended in time and become part of a vibrant tapestry of nostalgic memories. The college years. A wedding day. The birth of a child. But for me and a handful of others, 1972 will always stand out.

My friends and I mugged for the camera as some of our

children captured us on film. Unlike 15 years ago, when we first reunited, we did not jostle for position and line up exactly as we did for our eighth-grade class picture.

We have, after all, grown up.

(Autumn 1997)

The Men of 1903 Trinity

With papers and final exams still to be tackled before graduation, 10 University of Dayton roommates and a dozen or so friends, many barefooted and clad in shorts, retreated to the tiny third-floor chapel in a campus house.

Welcome to the weekly 9 p.m. Mass on Mondays at 1903 Trinity Ave., an oasis of tranquility in the middle of what can be a raucous college student neighborhood.

"I know these are your last days," said Father Ignase "Iggy" Arulappen, standing behind a simple altar flanked by two candles. "Many times we read in the newspaper all that is bad in our world. We hear less about the grace of God. (The world) needs the eyes of grace and faith to see."

My son Ali and his friends sat cross-legged on the floor and prayed for the recovery of one of the roommates' aunts, an end to school gun violence and the safety of the people of Nicaragua caught up in bloody anti-government protests. During the traditional sign of peace, the students embraced everyone in the room in a tender moment that lingered.

Afterward, Ali said, "This is a time to take a breath, feel peace and feel the human touch."

It's also a bittersweet time for my son and his roommates, who lived together "in community," to use the Marianist lingo, over two years in special student houses in UD's neighborhood. An eclectic group, they hail from different parts of the country — from Pittsburgh and Atlanta to Fort Wayne and Cincinnati. One is Chinese. My son is a Muslim.

They shared meals and prayed together. They bared their souls about tough professors and broken relationships, divisiveness in the country and hopes for humanity. They challenged their neighbors to a crock-pot cook-off and invited other students over for dinner and roundtable discussions every single week. They took turns tending to the demands of an energetic puppy. Some spent their summers in a dilapidated farmhouse in Appalachia, living among the people of Salyersville, Kentucky.

Armed with degrees in fields as diverse as electrical engineering and English, all worried what the uncertain future held for them.

As their days together wound down, one joked, "We'll never live in a 10-bedroom house again in our lives," leaving unsaid that the bond of friendship that unites them today will be harder to maintain when they move the last couch out and move on to new lives. In preparation, they've scrawled a to-do list on a kitchen blackboard. On one side: "Clean fridge, empty closets, vacuum/mop, bathrooms!!!" On the other: "Solve world hunger."

I flash back to the words of Father Jim Schimelpfening at first-year orientation Mass at UD Arena nearly four years ago: "I hope you learn how to ask questions, the questions that really make a difference, the questions that change lives," he said.

"Who do you say you are? How you answer that question sets the stage for everything."

If graduation is the ultimate final exam, these guys may have aced the answer to that question.

Ali is heading to NYU to earn a graduate degree in social work and turn his passion for helping troubled youth into a profession. Others are studying theology and medicine or taking jobs in engineering and finance. One has signed up for a year of service in Chicago with Precious Blood Ministry of Reconciliation, which works to help children and families heal and rebuild after violence and conflict.

All seven graduating seniors are taking University of Dayton President Eric Spina's charge at the spring commencement ceremony to heart: "Do not use your degree just to make a living. Use your degree to make a difference."

(Spring 2018)

The Joe Belle Story

I borrowed Mitch Albom's book *Tuesdays with Morrie*, but I don't need to read it.

That's because I know Joe Belle, who has given everyone he has touched in the past year an indelible lesson in how to live life. It's a primer on how to remain unflinching when faced with insurmountable odds and faith-filled when faith is the only cure.

He describes the ups and downs of living with an incurable disease as "wacky." He euphemistically calls his 13-month battle with recurring brain tumors "the Joe Belle story." In his heart, he knows his story is inspirational. The Joe Belle story is about how to live every moment as if it were your last one, how to live without regrets. How to live.

"He gives you 200, 300 percent," said University of Dayton President Brother Raymond L. Fitz when he gave Belle UD's Lackner Award for advancing the Catholic and Marianist character of campus over three decades — first as an undergraduate student from the Bronx, then as an administrator in the student development division.

Some people stay in bed for two days with a cold, but Belle's Italian grandparents instilled in him a strong immigrant work ethic: "You get to church and you get to school," he's fond of saying. That's why he's back at work two days after a seizure or an all-day Gamma Knife procedure that uses intense radiation to attack tumors. In 26 years, the unflappable Belle hadn't missed a day of work until he underwent a delicate operation to remove an aggressive cancerous tumor in his brain.

I've nicknamed him Cal Ripken. I've labeled him the Energizer bunny. I've described him as an inspiration. But mostly I've called him a friend.

Countless others also love him and call him friend. Countless more are inspired — amazed, even — by his open-book approach to a marathon that has tested his body but not his will. All are moved by his family's courage and faith.

When the *Dayton Daily News* featured him in a front-page story, letters and phone calls poured in. His e-journal keeps relatives, friends and other brain tumor patients informed of his progress and educated about a disease that rammed into his life with the speed of a freight train.

Belle's candor and take-charge attitude don't surprise anyone. That's just Joe.

"When I think of Joe, I have two strong images. I see a man walking across campus at a speed no one else can match, and I see him working the crowd, but not in an egotistical way," said Bill Schuerman, vice president of student development at the University of Dayton and a close friend. "He's always shaking someone's hand, patting someone on the back. When Joe got this disease, he didn't stop working the crowd."

Today, that crowd is praying for a miracle while listening to the comeback kid talk about the options, amuse us with his quips, strengthen us with his resolve. A third tumor tripled in size, growing too close to the cerebellum for his neurosurgeon to operate. He's undergoing his sixth cycle of chemotherapy.

Despite it all, he has continued to choreograph his life — from taking the annual "male bonding" trip to an out-of-state Dayton Flyers basketball game and overseeing construction of a new apartment building on campus to telling the people he cares about what they mean to him.

That's not unusual. Many people do that when faced with their mortality. Joe has always done that.

"Whenever you worry about Joe and how he's doing, he worries about you," said Bruce Duke, a neighbor and colleague who has driven Belle to work for months. "That's a gift. Joe has a gift for living."

He's teaching us all how to live.

(Summer 2000)

Postscript: Joe Belle died July 9, 2000, at the age of 50, but not before gathering family and friends at his home around his bedside for a toast. We shared stories and our love. We laughed and cried, but mostly we felt the warm embrace of a moment none of us will ever forget. For his funeral Mass, I served as a pallbearer, the only woman bestowed with this honor. Joe is buried at Woodland Cemetery on a site that overlooks the campus he loved.

MOTHERHOOD

It's Not About Me

We've known the truth for a while, but the words stick in the throat.

"It's not about me."

Over a bottle of wine and mugs of coffee during a long-over-due visit, my college roommate and I watched the fireflies light up the trees like twinkling Christmas lights and finally blurted out the truth our mothers knew long before it dawned on us.

"It's not about me."

When Denise and I shared a house with Toni during our senior year in college, we'd sit at the kitchen table long into the night and talk about our dreams, our desires, our destinies.

We were our mothers' daughters by blood, not ambition. Kids would not tie us down. We would not lose our spontaneity. We would shape our futures, much like we carefully scheduled our college classes around our "real" lives.

For a while, we clung stubbornly to our idealism. When I landed an overseas journalism internship with McGraw-Hill World News in London, Denise and Toni jumped at the adventure of being stowaways on an international journey.

College degrees in hand, no job prospects in sight. Little money. Cheap standby airline tickets out of New York's immense JFK International Airport. Our suitcases crammed with clothes and hearts buoyed by youthful confidence, we were in search of the stuff dreams are made of, the kinds of memories that fuel friendships that last well beyond college.

"The first time I ever ate marmalade, real marmalade, was

at Edith's bed-and-breakfast in London," Denise remembered. Toni and I both fell in love with men with accents, imported them, married them.

Life was about us. Marmalade or men. We went after what we wanted.

Fast forward two decades. At middle age, we're changing diapers, maneuvering around toys in driveways that look like giant obstacle courses, putting careers on hold or in neutral, worrying about the health of our aging parents, watching seemingly endless Little League games, trying to balance our lives without losing ourselves.

"It's not about me," I heard myself concede in exasperation as we swatted at the mosquitoes and listened to the melodic lullaby of the crickets from the front-yard swing.

In college, I drank coffee out of a well-worn *The Young and the Restless* mug and wore a nightshirt proclaiming, "I want my space … and his, too." Like a boundless highway, the days stretched before me with endless possibilities. Today, I carefully choreograph the schedules of a family of four. Sometimes the only hour of the week where I'm truly alone is in church.

But I'm not alone. My friends lead the same crazed lives, occasionally pausing to reflect on the passage of time, on whether dreams have been deferred or have simply changed shape because of the constant battle of balancing family and career — without seeing your sense of self swallowed in the process.

I never expected to be changing diapers in my 40s or feeling such a strong sense of accomplishment from coaxing a blue sno-cone stain out of a toddler's white shirt. I never thought that one day my parents might depend upon me as I once depended upon them. I've learned to take delight in the small stuff: hearing the 2-year-old belt out the refrain from the Rolling Stones' classic,

"I Can't (Get No) Satisfaction," admiring the 8-year-old's headfirst slide into third base, watching my mother slowly, triumphantly lift her right arm paralyzed from a stroke.

Before my college roommate loads the kids in the car, we take a morning walk along a country road. "Look at that green dragon," says her 2-year-old son, wonder in his voice. A dragonfly flits across a creek. We laugh at his innocence and remember ours.

As I watched our children scamper, the realization hits me without regret: This is the stuff dreams are made of.

Maybe it is about me after all.

(Autumn 1999)

Momsick

Leaving traffic-choked streets, we pulled into a quiet cemetery on the outskirts of the Pakistani city of Lahore. A dozen of us filed along a rocky path to a newly dug grave, lit incense and silently, tearfully prayed. Our grief lingered like the incense.

The mosque and playground sitting just inside the cemetery's ornate gate — symbols of faith and family — perfectly portray Apa, who was more than just the matriarch of this close-knit Pakistani family. She was the heart and soul.

Just days before my husband, Zafar, and our sons were to embark on our annual summer trip to Lahore, we received word that Apa, his mother, had died suddenly of a heart attack. The timing gutted us all.

Earlier that summer, I had decided to quit wrestling with fear and heed the U.S. government's warning to avoid travel to Pakistan, where anti-American sentiment was running high. With the world on high terror alert, Pakistan's ruling military general, Pervez Musharraf, continued to arrest Taliban and al-Qaeda supporters as well as mullahs who preached hate. For an American, this sun-drenched country along the Arabian Sea was not a tourist hot spot.

Yet when Apa died, my anxiety evaporated. Love trumps fear.

Everyone — from her five devoted sons to the family's servants — called her Apa, Urdu for "sister." With sisterly concern, she worried about the lives of all she touched. As I reflect on her life, she was one of the most courageous, generous women I've ever known.

During the turbulent partition of the subcontinent nearly six decades earlier, she left an opulent life in a Mughal-style mansion in Samana, India, to climb onto a train that was packed with Muslims fleeing for their safety. Married with three small boys, she sacrificed a life rich in the material sense for the promise of one richer — a secure harbor in a brand-new country where her family members could practice their religion without fear.

Apa's tightly woven family — three generations living together under the same roof — adored her. Her formal schooling ended after fifth grade, but she devoured the newspaper daily and dispensed wisdom and compassion gained from a life that, by the family's math, had spanned at least 85 years. She had no birth certificate.

My husband has always teased me, "You're No. 1 in your category," and I've never resented his unconditional, deep love for his mother, despite my rocky beginning in her life. When he phoned her from London in 1982 with the bombshell that he wanted to marry an American, her words cut through him, "You're no longer my son."

After all, as part of Muslim tradition, she found wives for her sons. No one had ever married outside the faith — or lived permanently outside the family home.

While Zafar rejected this preordained destiny, he never turned his back on her. After numerous phone calls, she reluctantly gave him her blessing when we agreed to travel to Lahore for the wedding.

For years, Zafar phoned her every Saturday morning. He taught his children that "heaven lies under your mother's feet." When Zafar's father died in 1998, we vowed to return every summer to visit her, a promise broken only the summer after 9/11.

I know a few words of Urdu. She knew little English. She was Muslim. I'm Christian.

Yet, over more than two decades, we built a rich relationship, bound by a mutual love for her son and the universal language of motherhood. Our sons, hardly angelic, could do no wrong in her eyes.

When I told these stories to a class at Wilmington College in Ohio, the students turned their attention away from whether Osama bin Laden was hiding along the Afghanistan-Pakistan border and peppered me with questions about my marriage and everyday life. What most Americans know of Pakistan can be summed up in the images we glimpse on CNN when a bomb explodes or a government collapses.

This country cherishes its children and reveres its elderly. In Pakistan, our boys play nightly pickup games with their cousins, their ears attuned to the melody of the ice cream truck. It's just like back home, only the game is cricket, not baseball.

Few Americans have experienced life in a Muslim country, and after Sept. 11, 2001, many turned inward. When President Bush told the world, "Either you're with us or you're against us," he rallied people around fighting terrorism and also contributed to a divide that continues to grow wider.

My marriage bridges two cultures and two religions in a world that is not as black and white as some paint it. As bombings in England illustrated, extremists can be found in any country — not just the ones we've deemed unsafe. Evidenced by the headlines in Pakistan's newspapers, its citizens fear terrorism as much as we do.

The United States should not lose its focus on fighting terrorism, but we also must work at nurturing what unites us. Over more than two decades, I've observed life in this impoverished, developing country and tried to write about our common humanity.

People like Apa don't make the news, yet their lives leave an enduring mark on those left behind. "She was our hope, our support," said her youngest son, Nadeem.

"When she died, I felt like I was 10 years old again," said her oldest son, Abid. "She was a mother to everyone," added her nephew Tanzeem.

When I arrived in Lahore a week after my family, our 9-year-old son Ali, in the way that only children can express emotions, said, "I thought I was homesick, but I was Momsick."

As we sorrowfully left the cemetery, we all felt the same way.

(Autumn 2005)

Remain Tall

When you juggle an at-times taxing career with carpooling, laundry and other unsung joys of motherhood, the last thing you need is a "homework" assignment from your child's school. Writing a heartfelt letter for a time capsule – something for an eighth grader to read in four years at high school graduation – may be the only exception.

Dear Qasim,

When you were a toddler, I used to gaze into your wide, brown, innocent eyes and imagine the man you would become. Today, as you finish eighth grade, I see the shadow of that man.

Within the last few months, you've inched taller than your parents, much to your delight. You don't even attempt to hide the twinkle in your eyes when you stand next to us and look down. You aspire to play high school basketball and continue to surprise us with the ease with which you launch a three-point shot. There's little fuss in your playing. You never pump your hand in the air when you hit a shot with a hand in your face.

You are not a person of great fanfare, and I admire that about you. No one appreciates a braggart. You've quietly and diligently worked hard this year to earn straight A's. We're enormously proud of your work ethic and attitude. Those traits will serve you well as you make your own way in the world.

Your growing love of traveling and discovering new cities will enable you to feel comfortable in a world that expands beyond your backyard. When you took a charter bus to Washington,

D.C., this spring with your class, you used your knowledge of the Underground in London to figure out how to travel on the Metro.

After 9/11, too many Americans quit looking outward out of fear and ignorance. But today it's more important than ever to open your heart to new experiences and different cultures. As you continue to travel, you will learn to be tolerant and flexible.

Peer pressure can cause us to march in lockstep. During a year of political polarization, you stepped out of conformity and worked on John Kerry's losing campaign for president. Most of your classmates supported George Bush, though few watched the presidential debates and scanned the polls as you did. You walked Vandalia's neighborhoods, passing out campaign literature and counting the lawn signs. We joined thousands of other supporters at a boisterous, energizing campaign rally in downtown Dayton.

When the boys in your class teased you about wearing your Kerry T-shirt and campaign pin to school, you didn't don a less controversial shirt. You didn't hide the pin. You didn't back down on your stance that the war in Iraq was immoral. You retaught me a lesson you'll keep learning throughout your life: If you believe strongly in something, be brave enough to state your convictions.

When I was in eighth grade at St. Chris, I developed a corps of friends who remain in my life today. Anthony, or "Antonio" as you've renamed him, became your eighth-grade buddy. You roomed together in D.C., and you taught him how to fix his basketball mechanics and improve his free throw percentage. He brought out your sense of humor. "Anthony is an ogre," you always joked about your shy, lanky friend. Bantering can become a term of endearment among friends, whom you will learn to treasure even more as you grow older.

When you read this letter, you'll be finishing up your last few days of high school and preparing for the unknown world of college. Your emotions will run the gamut from excitement to fear.

Look in the mirror and remember the man that began to emerge in eighth grade. Remain tall in your own eyes and believe in yourself as we have always believed in you. Use your mind — fully. Maintain a positive attitude, even in the face of disappointment and loss. Reach out to your friends and family, who are always in your corner. Don't be afraid to lose. It's a part of life.

Have faith in yourself and in your future. You are a gift to us — and the world. We will always love you.

Love,
Mom

(Summer 2005)

Born to be a Flyer

I sort through photos, ticket stubs, report cards, news clippings.

The memories wash over me like high tide, and I struggle to stay afloat above a mother's emotions of watching her child turn into a man.

This winter, after learning you'd been accepted to the University of Dayton, we pulled into the arena for a Dayton Flyers game, and you acknowledged with quiet pride and a touch of wonder, "I've been going to games all my life, and I'm finally a member of the Flyer family."

But you've always been a Flyer. I learned I was pregnant just days after earning a master's degree in English from the university. Seconds after phoning your father, I blurted the news to my colleagues in UD's public relations office. Over the years, they've endured stories of your love for the Flyers and your own exploits on the court, including a play-by-play analysis of how you came off the bench in the seventh grade and shot the lights out, leading your struggling team to its first win of the season.

You learned to count and make colorful "masterpieces" at the child care center on campus. You mastered the back float at the Physical Activities Center. You earned "Camper of the Year" honors at the Oliver Purnell basketball camp. Your drawers are full of Flyer T-shirts. Dayton Flyer floor mats grace the floor of your Toyota. One spring, a high school guidance counselor knocked on the door of your honors English class, grinned and flashed the score of the Flyers' Atlantic 10 tourney game directly at you. Your teacher was not amused.

Now, as you graduate from high school, you hesitate, not knowing quite what to expect.

Here's a little secret to college: It's not about earning a degree. It's about making a life. Your life. Not what anyone else wants for you, but what you want for yourself.

You will discover your gifts, what brings you joy.

You will conquer your fears, taking risks you never thought possible. Maybe you'll spend a summer on a service project in an impoverished village in Guatemala or push yourself to perform in a class that stretches you. A professor will open your mind in ways you never imagined.

You will make countless new friends. Your heart may break, but you will learn, over time, that you're resilient. And love will come again when you least expect it.

In four years, you will wonder how your college years evaporated so quickly. One minute you're part of the infamous Red Scare student fan section, screaming, "We are UD!" In the next minute, you'll be hearing the stirring refrains of the University of Dayton "Anthem" at your graduation ceremony.

Listen to those words, rising and falling in the distance.

"Your alma mater calls. UD, we hear you calling."

(Summer 2009)

Mischief Dances in His Eyes

(The time capsule homework project, the sequel. As I did for Qasim, I shared memories, hopes and dreams in a letter tucked in a time capsule that Ali opened on the eve of his high school graduation.)

Dear Ali,

One of your uncles once had this to say about you: "Mischief dances in his eyes."

As you wrap up eighth grade and prepare to enter high school, we jokingly say the jury is still out on whether you're going to use your immense charm for good or evil. We are *kidding*, of course.

Your potential for greatness far outweighs your occasional tendency to get yourself in the doghouse. You are one of the most affectionate and intelligent people I know, with a curiosity about the world and spontaneity for life that cannot be taught from a textbook. You have charisma. These are your inborn traits that will take you far in life.

From the moment you were born, you've had the power to amuse those around you. You brought so much joy to your grandmothers — one in the U.S., the other in Pakistan — with your antics. Though you have no desire to be an actor, you get a kick out of making us laugh by slipping into an Australian or Indian accent at will.

Do you remember this crazy and imaginative exchange we once had? Everyone knows you shouldn't accept a ride from a stranger, but you thought there must be at least one exception to this rule. "If I were lost in the woods with no one around and a limousine pulled up, *would it be acceptable* to have a limousine ride?" you asked as I drove you to school.

You're very quotable, a writer's dream. That's why your words have ended up in pieces I've published. I often wish I carried a notebook to record your witty, frequently absurd observations.

You solved this dilemma yourself by tackling your "memoir" one snowy week and writing notes in your iPod about the clever things you've said. Like the time I tried vainly to remember one of your amusing phrases. "It begins with F," I kept insisting. Worn down, you replied in exasperation, "Mom, think outside the F!" Later, you typed into your iPod the words I couldn't retain, "I'm flourishing in my awesomeness!"

Today, as you open this letter on the eve of your high school graduation, you are ready to flourish. You face a future you will create.

Remember to be tolerant and respectful of others. You've traveled the world — visiting both mosques and topless beaches during one memorable summer spent partly in an Islamic country and partly on the French Riviera.

Your parents honor two religions and grew up in two cultures. Always try to see the other person's point of view. Even though as a family we're vocal about politics around the dinner table, not everyone you'll stumble across in life shares the same perspectives. Listen to others, even if you disagree.

Be brave. Don't be afraid to wander outside your comfort zone. Push yourself to succeed. You may fail, but you will never know the sweetness of success unless you try. Don't give in to the tendency to blame others. Always accept responsibility — and never give up on your dreams. Set your own goals and work to meet them.

Most importantly, remember who you are. Rein in your

impulsiveness, but be spontaneous. Continue to bring immense joy to those around you. Be curious about the world. Use your imagination. Be loving.

And never forget how much we love you — and always will. You are an exceptional person, and we are blessed to have you in our lives.

Love,
Mom

(Summer 2010)

Voyages

After I helped you move a few clothes, a coffee pot and some cherished books into your Marycrest Hall room, I unfolded a letter you wrote to us last spring.

"Now is a crucial time to voyage off to a new world full of wonder and spirituality," you wrote in an unsuccessful attempt to persuade us to allow you to travel to Tibet to study with the monks for a few months before college. You were just 17 and already expressing a curiosity about the world and your place in it.

You have an inquisitiveness and a spontaneity for life that books alone cannot teach. Some would say you're overly confident and too impulsive. You've always believed you have all the answers and certainly know the exceptions to the rules. You skirted that line with your teachers throughout school.

Yet as you started your first year at the University of Dayton, you found yourself full of questions. And you were worried.

"You're 18 and you don't know what you want to do? That's the best thing I've heard you say," political science professor Mark Ensalaco told you over lunch. "Ask tough questions," he advised. "We need more people asking excellent questions instead of giving meaningless answers."

In your first few weeks as a college student, you read Mike Rose's essay "I Just Want to Be Average" in Margaret Strain's writing seminar, and it opened your eyes to how one person who believes in you can change your life.

You helped your Saudi Arabian roommate write a paper. As part of the social justice learning-living community in Marycrest

Complex, you traveled to Edison School to tutor a fourth grader in basic arithmetic.

You're already exploring study-abroad options in Africa, yet you are quick to grab a Nerf gun for stress-relieving, heated battles that break out randomly on the dorm's second floor.

And while you're not Catholic, you were visibly moved by the words of Father Jim Schimelpfening during first-year orientation Mass at UD Arena. "I hope you learn how to ask questions, the questions that really make a difference, the questions that change lives," he said.

"We're not a world at peace. Are you willing to be a peacemaker? We're not a world with universal health care. Are you willing to hear the cry of the poor and be the voice for the voiceless? Who do you say you are? How you answer that question sets the stage for everything."

Who do you say you are?

The answer isn't part of a pop quiz in physics. It won't jump off the page of a reading assignment.

It's a question that will weave through every class, every friendship, every experience during your college days — and beyond.

It's time for you to voyage to a world you will create, a new world full of wonder.

(Winter 2014)

SPORTS,
THE GREAT
METAPHOR

The Joy of T-ball

There's a 6-year-old on my T-ball team whose arm reportedly rivals that of a Cy Young winner.

"Randy Johnson throws almost as good as Zach," marvels my son Ali.

As a first-time T-ball manager, I've rediscovered something more fundamental than the fundamentals of this sport that's designed to prepare kindergartners and first graders for baseball.

When you're small, you tend to think big.

You're not afraid of failure.

You play for the exhilaration of playing.

You always win.

At lunch with other 40-something professionals, a woman I just met impressed me with her poise and humor, then offered a surprising confession: "My 5-year-old has more presence and confidence than I think I've ever had."

When I interviewed the late Hans von Ohain, co-inventor of the jet engine, he chuckled at his youthful confidence. "I didn't even consider any possibility of failure," he said. "Today, whenever I have a new thought, I think of potential failure because I don't want to overlook anything. When you're an old man, you can't play like a young man."

Staring middle age resolutely in the face, some women take up marathon running. Others embark on second careers. (Who doesn't know someone who's suddenly become a massage therapist?) I've turned into "Coach Mom" with a car trunk full of bats, balls and bases.

As I watch the ball roll through their gloves and the tee sail to the pitcher's mound during a Monday night practice, I notice that the lack of experience does not dampen the eagerness in these pint-sized boys of summer. "Can I play first base? Can I play first base? Can I play first base?" one beseeches. "Sure, go ahead," I respond, stirred by his persistence.

"Where is it?" he asks.

Stifling a laugh, I wonder when we start to play it safe. When do some of us start doing a strengths-and-weaknesses analysis every time we're faced with a new challenge or tasked with an unfamiliar role?

"Maybe it happens when you get evaluated over and over by coaches, fans, parents, bosses. Eventually that may change your positive approach from innovative to more guarded and unimaginative," says University of Dayton psychology professor Charles Kimble, who studies self-handicapping — the tendency of some people to inadequately prepare for important tasks so that they have a built-in excuse if they fail.

University of Dayton management professor Dean McFarlin speculates that age 8 may be a turning point. "I once asked my son's third grade teacher, who was fantastic, why she didn't teach a different grade. She said, 'It's about as old as (students) go without losing that wide-eyed look.'"

I once took a "coaching" workshop to learn how to transform myself from a boss to a coach in my day job. It was all about building a competitive edge and developing "high-performance" teams. Consultant Thomas Crane urged managers to coach from the heart and create an environment where people do not hold back because they're afraid to fail.

Perhaps such professional development workshops should include an hour on the T-ball field, where there's no shortage of heart and hustle. These boys approach the game with innocence, earnestness — and irrepressible optimism.

They remind you the secret to a fulfilling life is not all that complicated. You show up. You play hard. You try not to throw your bat. You have fun.

"What did you think of our first game?" I ask my son, looking for affirmation about our debut together on the playing field. "It was sweet!" he answered, his eyes full of joy.

(Summer 2009)

A Point Guard in the Game of Life

It's not unusual to spot Edwin Young perched on a ladder as he lowers a basketball net.

The rim may be closer to the hardwood, but his expectations remain high.

"This is basketball," he yells to a scrappy group of 10-year-olds during a scrimmage game, clapping his hands in rapid staccato fashion. "Have your hands up and ready to play. Be ready to play every second. Push it. Push it. Push it."

They raise the intensity level, scrambling after every loose ball as if this were a March Madness contest instead of an end-of-practice pick-up game.

At 6 feet, 2 inches tall, Young towers over these elementary school kids. When he was their age, he pretended to be Magic Johnson and shot baskets every night at a rec center in his California neighborhood. As point guard for the Dayton Flyers, he led the surging team to the NCAA playoffs with tenacious play and a smothering brand of defense that earned him the nickname "The Blanket."

He no longer plays before 13,000 screaming fans at the University of Dayton Arena, where he enjoyed raising the decibel level by waving his arms skyward. He no longer harbors hopes of playing professional basketball, though he had an opportunity to run the offense for a team in Lyon, France.

Today, he instills the dream in young kids.

"These kids know I played, but I don't want them to think I was some hero. I don't want to live in the past," he says. "If I was by myself, I would have taken that chance and gone to Europe, but I had to think about my family. I had to weigh my odds. I played for 20 years, and it was time to hang up my shoes. I got a $75,000 scholarship from basketball, I'm free of debt, and I needed to move on in my life."

He's adjusted his game. By day, he dons a suit and tie and works as a financial consultant for Merrill Lynch. By night, he coaches the Dayton Warriors, a fourth-grade select basketball team, schooling them in the fundamentals — and more. He drills them in layups, jump shots, free throws, man-to-man defense, slowly pulling out their potential. Meanwhile, assistant coach Tony Bennett quizzes the kids on how they're doing in school. "It's habit," says Bennett, an assistant academic coordinator for the Flyers.

As a star in college, Young set a school record by knocking down 18 straight free throws in a game. It's no surprise to find his team at the line, shooting endless foul shots at the end of practice when they're exhausted. It's a game situation.

But for Young, basketball is not just a game. It's a metaphor for life.

"He says to play hard every minute," says my son Qasim, who's on the team. Then he quickly corrects himself: "No, he says to play hard every second. He always says never give up. Always play hard."

Those are words to live by. I can't recall much about high school calculus, but I remember everything I learned on the ball diamond and the tennis court. You develop tenacity, you learn teamwork, you push yourself to your potential, you care about results. And you fall back on those skills every day of your life. There are no practice games. I repeatedly share these lessons with my son, but Qasim actually lives them when he plays for Young.

A fierce competitor, Young doesn't judge his team's success on wins and losses. He's obsessed with improvement. "Instead of dribbling with their heads down, I want to see them dribble with their heads up and call plays. I don't care if they throw up air balls. They have to play hard for their team."

At a downtown gym two days after a heartbreaking one-point loss, the Warriors battle back in their next contest.

They dribble with their heads up. They look for the open teammate.

They play hard every minute. Every second.

After all, this is more than basketball. And with less than a minute on the clock, Young's boys hang on to a slender three-point lead for a hard-fought win.

Lessons learned.

(Spring 2001)

Fair Game

When we rounded up every kid in the neighborhood for base-ball games on muggy summer nights, at least our silly, made-up childhood rules had a purpose.

I quit pulling the ball to left field after workers erected a huge water tower smack in left-center field of the small grassy park near our house. We did away with the left fielder, and any ball hit left of the water tower was an automatic out. Since we rarely fielded enough people to play every position, these seemed like logical rules.

The field used by the coed softball league at Ohio University doesn't sport a huge, mushroom-shaped water tower to use as a scapegoat — or a convenient excuse — for the league's inane rules.

I guess whoever devised the rules thought they were fair ones. After all, even in this day and age of The Assertive Woman, we all know a woman can't hit or pitch, right?

At first glance, the rules look reasonable. Under the coed decree, you send as many women out into the field as men, or you forfeit. That's fair.

Then it gets strange.

At least two of The Fairer Sex play in the infield, but not as either pitcher or catcher. Just when I think I've finally mastered the slow-pitch arc after six summers of pitching in competitive leagues, I'm denied the opportunity to show it off for my teammates.

But that's not what's so frustrating. All the guys bat oppo-site-handed because apparently half of the team in the field can't field, either. Carry this silliness just a step further: If one of your male teammates walks because the pitches are wild, or he's never been able to bat left-handed and saves face by waiting for four balls, the woman on deck walks, too.

Sure, when you're down by two, the bases are loaded and your male teammate has worked a 3-2 count, it's tempting to yell, "Wait on it!" Two walks for the price of one. That's just common-sense strategy.

It's also sexist, archaic and exasperating.

As kids playing baseball every night of our childhood, we dragged everyone we could find to the park after dinner. The least talented players, regardless of gender, were always chosen last.

That's the way it ought to be in intramural softball, too. Everyone should be given an equal opportunity to play, under no special rules (except for a water tower clause).

Just five men, five women — and the worst player in right field. Game on.

(Spring 1980)

The Girls of Winter

Like most brainstorms-turned-catastrophes, it sounded like a great idea at the time.

A double-elimination softball tournament. All proceeds donated to the March of Dimes. A chance to compete in a sport we all love and help a good cause at the same time. If only it hadn't been in the winter.

"You'll love it," team captain Barb Billings said enthusiastically two weeks before The Big Event.

But two days before The Big Event, Billings was desperately trying to find 10 people foolish enough to don scarves, gloves and long underwear to play a summer sport on a frozen field on a frosty February morning.

"I don't know why nobody sounds enthused anymore," she complained. "Wear layers of clothes and your winter coat — and expect to really hurt the next day. Last year I couldn't even lift my coffee cup, that's how much pain I was in."

A true lover of the game, I've played ball under all sorts of adversities. A friend and I used to literally "warm up" in a church parking lot during blustery winter recesses to get in shape for the upcoming season. I survived a spring of coed intramural soft-ball at Ohio University where the crazy sexist rules were slanted in favor of each of the team's mandatory five female players. Even though it was illegal to strike out, it wasn't much fun. And during neighborhood games played nearly every humid summer night during my youth, a true athlete learned to play the ball off the red-and-white mushroom-shaped water tower looming in left-center field.

Still, I felt my enthusiasm waning when I heard the National Weather Service's winter storm warning and learned the temperature was a frigid 11 degrees two hours before game time. I worried about frostbite. I worried about being able to pitch a 10-foot arc with gloves on and no practice since August. The whole idea was beginning to sound silly.

"Let's lose our two and get out of here," quipped catcher Judy Knopps during pregame warm-ups. "We just wanted to say we played, didn't we?"

It was one thing trying to jam feet fitted with four pairs of socks into Nikes that morning, but that was nothing compared to the worries I'd encounter at game time. Playing on a frozen field tufted with uneven patches of snow and moon-like craters was "like playing on concrete," shortstop Billings grumbled after a fruitless first inning of bad bounces.

We named our team the Fusiliers, which first baseman Diane Hertlein said meant "fused together for the same cause," though some benchwarmers translated it as French for "fools." Under coatless coach Bob Colton, we rallied to barely lose the first game 9-8 to a scrappy team called Good Times.

After lunch, we arrived back to the field to discover the temperature had warmed into the upper 20s, a veritable heat wave enough to transform the field into a muddy swamp.

"This is dry compared to last year," Knopps said as she surveyed the slushy diamond. "The mud came up to our shins then, and they had to move the games to the grass."

It's not easy to pitch a mud-soaked ball from an imaginary pitching rubber situated between two puddles. It's not easy and can be downright embarrassing to field a ball that skids by you and sticks in the ground. Suddenly, sno-ball had turned into mud ball and the game into a comedy of errors. The Fusiliers fizzled out to another one-run loss, 8-7, to Trapper's Troopers.

"These Americans are weird, don't you agree?" asked my Asian-born husband as I dragged my weary, muddy body into the car. "That's a silly, mad game."

Not in the springtime, I thought. But in the mud and snow, yes, it was.

(Winter 1983)

A Game Plan for Life

Like many parents of my generation, I find myself running from soccer field to school gym to baseball diamond as my 7-year-old chases soccer balls, shoots the jumper and jogs around the bases.

He thrives on the thrill of competition and harbors hopes of making the NBA someday — never mind that neither of his parents could reach 5 feet, 8 inches on tiptoe. He loves to sing, "I Believe I Can Fly."

A parent never expects a child's dreams to die, to turn into a family's nightmare. On an unseasonably warm Sunday in Lent, Stacey Martin's grief-stricken soccer teammates gathered in the University of Dayton's Immaculate Conception Chapel to mourn the loss of the team's junior fullback. As her parents watched her compete in a spring exhibition game a day earlier, the athlete with "the ever-present smile and sparkling eyes" collapsed and, inexplicably, died.

As a campus community, we had not finished grieving for Flyer basketball star Chris Daniels, a gentle giant who died in 1996 of cardiac arrhythmia, nor Benjamin Columbus, the 15-year-old son of *University of Dayton Quarterly* editor Tom Columbus who died while warming up before soccer practice a few months later.

As the mother of a budding athlete, I find it painful to even imagine how parents and friends begin to heal when a youth dies without warning. The frailty of life is beyond our comprehension when it involves those who have not yet learned to drive, earned a college diploma, fallen in love with a kindred spirit.

Do we forget the overwhelming odds of such a tragedy

happening? Do we give in to irrational worry and pull our children off the field?

At a prayer and healing service two days after Stacey's death, Father Gene Contadino tried to allay the fears in our hearts by using a sports analogy. "It's hard for us because we don't understand," he said quietly. "We want to scream, 'Why did you (God) take her out (of the game)? We need her.'"

He reminded us we can't retreat to the bench; we can't surrender to our trepidation. "We don't know about the last five minutes of her life, but we do know she was doing what she loved to do," he said. "If we could choose, you and I would die doing the things we loved."

As I watch my office colleague and friend struggle with the loss of his youngest son and keep his faith in a "coach" who mysteriously took his boy out of the game in the springtime of his life, I know that Tom has come to believe those words and find some measure of peace.

Like Stacey's tearful teammates who vowed, "We're going to mention her every day, at every game, at every practice," he will cherish Ben's memory every day for the rest of his life.

And some of Tom's best memories are as a spectator, watching his son's prowess on the soccer field and his grit on the basketball court while marveling at his youthful, can-do spirit. As with Stacey, Ben died on his field of dreams, doing what he loved best.

In retrospect, maybe that's a parent's best game plan — to allow our children to follow their hearts, to indulge in their youthful dreams, to help them deal with the inevitable wins and losses, on and off the field.

We need to be people of enough faith that we can swallow our fears and give our children the freedom to find their way in the world.

Unlike his teammates, who prefer to drive to the basket for the easy layup, my son launches a difficult fadeaway jumper. As the shot miraculously swishes through the net, he looks toward the stands to catch our eyes and smile, then hustles down the court.

For a flicker of a moment, I see the spirit of Stacey, Chris and Ben living in a little boy who believes he can fly.

(Summer 1998)

LIFE

AND

DEATH

A Journey of the Heart

This vacation won't be a day on the beach. In the wake of nuclear tests and random bombings and shootings, the State Department is warning Americans to curtail nonessential travel to Pakistan.

Our family is ignoring the warnings and the headlines and making a pilgrimage to Pakistan this summer. We're following the advice of the wise fox in the timeless children's classic *The Little Prince:* "It is only with the heart that one can see rightly; what is essential is invisible to the eye."

My husband's father, whose health had started to fail as we were trying to get our passports in order, has died. Although it's too late for the funeral, we want to be there for Chehlum, the traditional Islamic day of praying and sharing of food with the poor on the 40th day after someone's death. It's essential we go.

"But isn't there a war there?" asks my father, who learns of the trip days after Pakistan announced it now has the atomic bomb and will not be bullied by neighboring foe India.

It's hard for Americans to understand the rationale behind the political turmoil between Pakistan and India. Why would two impoverished countries embark on a costly nuclear arms race? Why pick at an open sore that won't heal?

It's hard, too, to understand why a country born out of a passion to create a free Islamic state would terrorize a faction of its own people. And why does the democratic government continue to collapse like a house of cards every few years?

Those are questions for the intellect, not the heart. As an American who has journeyed to Southeast Asia numerous times,

I have come to appreciate the life beyond the headlines. Pakistan's essential character is invisible to the eyes of most Americans, who typically don't tour developing countries.

This is a country that cherishes its children. In turn, children revere their parents.

I appreciate the deep bond and unconditional love my husband has for a family halfway around the world. Even though he's lived in the United States or England more than half of his life, he's more connected to his family than many Americans who live in the same area code as their relatives. That's why his father's death shook him to the depths of his soul.

In America, people struggle with the issue of caring for their elderly parents and grandparents. It's a nonissue in Pakistan, a country poor in the materialist sense but rich in heart. Most parents live with their sons and their families under one roof. They share meals, pickup games of cricket in the yard — and their lives.

Zafar's father, a retired police officer whose gentle manner belied the nature of his profession, adored the dozen grandchildren who would gallop through the house with youthful energy, oblivious to the 115-degree heat that blankets Lahore in the summer like a gigantic comforter.

A half-dozen framed pictures of our 7-year-old adorn his bedroom, a mini-shrine to a grandson growing up out of sight of his watchful, loving eyes. When I think of Aba Jee — a name meaning "dearest father" — I see a man casually resting on a hand-woven hammock in the early-morning sun, eating an orange and chatting with a child.

Aba Jee never bottled up his emotions, never hid his joy or sorrow. When we arrived for periodic three-week visits, he cried. When we left, he cried. He was always ready with a rambunctious bear hug for Qasim and a loud cry, "mera beta," meaning "my son."

As I watch my husband struggle with his father's death, I see the man's legacy. He tells his sons every day he loves them. He hugs and kisses them freely. He tells them there's one fact that's indisputable: They're not going to heaven unless they're good to their mother. When his father died, he cried — and they felt his pain.

Despite the miles, despite the political instability, despite the heat, we're going back.

It's essential.

(Summer 1998)

My Nanaw's Priceless Gifts

I picked up the Christmas card from Lincoln, Nebraska, and read the still-legible, scrawling handwriting of a 97-year-old woman I had never met.

"Have a good year as we close off a century of happy associations. God bless you. Love, Claire."

My eyes blurred with sudden tears, and my head dropped to the railing of my grandmother's bed, where Nanaw lay half-comatose, tethered to oxygen and holding onto a wisp of life even thinner than her white hair.

I unfolded another letter, this one to me from Nanaw's childhood friend, Viola King. The two had grown up together in the old Ohio Soldiers' and Sailors' Orphans' Home in Xenia, Ohio, forging the sort of family ties neither girl had ever had. During the five years Nanaw spent losing the battle to Parkinson's disease at Mercy Siena Woods nursing home, I read her letters and cards from friends whose names I had only seen on Christmas cards that I glanced at with vague curiosity.

Viola stood out among them, faithfully scribbling out long, chatty letters filled with tales from the past — both to my grandmother and to me, as I tried in vain to keep up with my end of Viola's correspondence. "Well, my dear friend, I no doubt have bored you enough — but I promise to keep on boring you," she vowed in one letter before launching into another amusing childhood memory. Another note included this P.S.: "Remember how I hated the nickname Skinny? Now I would love it."

As I reread the stack of letters from Viola found in my

grandmother's bedside table, I found myself smiling at the memories and appreciating the shared moments between two women who probably knew more about each other than even their husbands did.

Ironically, both men were named Fred. Just days before her best friend took her last breath, Viola wrote, "She helped me over the horrible period of my Fred's death, then I know I helped her after her Fred's death. So few people can have a lifetime friend. She was dearer to me than any member of my family."

When I was in college, my grandmother routinely sent me tuition and book money so that I could concentrate on developing skills as a journalist rather than backup skills as a waitress. I paid her back in envelopes of bylined articles that she shipped around to friends, much like chain letters.

She made down payments on houses for my brother and sister. She gave my father the business he and my grandfather started. She gave her friends and family loyalty, love, laughter.

Her around-the-clock nursing care ate up all of her savings, but she gave me a legacy far greater than any inheritance. She taught me the importance of cultivating friendships that can last a lifetime, the kind that bring memories of nearly "a century of happy associations." May we all be so lucky.

(Winter 1999)

The Godfather of Vandalia

Father Jim Fitz carried his vestments into my family's church on a humid July morning to help celebrate the life of my father, a man he had never met.

A longtime colleague of mine at the University of Dayton, Father Jim didn't call the parish priest in advance. He simply showed up. The Marianists always seem to know when you need their gentle presence the most.

My 80-year-old father would have loved that, just as he would have gotten a kick out of the police officer solemnly saluting the funeral procession winding through the tiny town of Vandalia, Ohio, where my father built a business and a life and raised four children who will never forget him.

For all who knew and loved him, Fred Krimm was simply unforgettable.

He was the "Godfather of Vandalia," the patriarch of our family, a generous and gregarious soul. He attended the University of Dayton for only one year before the U.S. Army drafted him to serve during the Korean War, so he learned about managing a small business the hard way — by doing.

He ran an ice cream store in Vandalia for nearly half a century, and everyone in town knew him.

"He used to get gas at Sohio back in the day," wrote Michael Criner on a Facebook page devoted to Vandalia memories. "(He) slid his credit card in the window and said, 'How ya doing, Lucky?' RIP, my smiling friend." Another wrote, "Another stone in the foundation of our youth has crumbled."

Others thanked him for giving them their first jobs. He gave me and my siblings our first paychecks, too. He taught us how to properly make and weigh creamy soft-serve cones and bake trays of huge soft pretzels. We knew never to ask for time off during the Dayton Air Show parade, the busiest night of the year.

When he learned that I was importing a husband from Pakistan, he uttered the infamous words, "I wish he had an oil well." Then he proceeded to call him "son" for the next 30 years.

My dad was not a complicated man. By example, he gave his children a strong work ethic and showed what it means to take your wedding vows to heart. He couldn't cook, do laundry or operate a microwave, but he stepped up and took care of our sick mother for a decade before she died nearly six years before him. He took her out to dinner and to get her hair done. He helped her to dress. He learned enough cooking skills to get by.

We feel blessed that he lived his life on his own terms right up to the last moment. He still barked orders from his chair at the Airline Dairy Creme every morning, still made the weekly trek to Lebanon, Ohio, to bet on the horses.

A few weeks before he died, he joined us for a simple Sunday supper of hamburgers and corn on the cob. A friend brought her family and 85-year-old father, and, true to form, my dad chatted away with Mary's dad as though they were best buddies.

It was a special moment that illuminated my father's life. The man did not know a stranger. He created bonds instantly, and he was loyal to his family and friends.

When waitresses, bank tellers — even a priest who never met you — pay their respects at your funeral, you've made a mark.

My dad lived a life worth celebrating.

(Autumn 2012)

A Legacy in Leaves

In February, my husband's early Valentine's Day gift arrived in a wheelbarrow.

I watched a red Japanese maple tree being planted in his mother's memory a few steps away from the sturdy tree that blooms for his father on the University of Dayton's campus.

"This is the best gift ever," he proclaimed.

Everyone — from her five devoted sons to the family's servants in Pakistan — had called her Apa, Urdu for "sister." A woman of wisdom, compassion and a lifelong quest for knowledge, she had lived at least 85 years, and her sudden death of a heart attack in 2005 just days before a family visit broke our hearts.

When I walk over to grab a quick lunch at the student union, I take a moment to brush aside the mulch covering the plaque under the graceful branches of a Pacific sunset maple tree. My father-in-law's legacy comes into focus: "In memory of Shahid Hussain Rizvi who dedicated his life for the betterment of his family and education."

Across the world in Lahore, Pakistan, my in-laws carefully tended the mango and date trees that stretched majestically above the walls that encircled the family home. During my first trip to Lahore, when Zafar and I married, they proudly showed off the famous Shalimar Gardens, centuries-old Mughal-style terraced gardens — a peaceful oasis in an often-turbulent country.

On campus, the chapel bells remind us of the power of faith. In Lahore, the lyrical Islamic call for prayer can be heard in the streets five times a day.

Two religions. Two vastly different cultures divided by nearly 8,000 miles. Yet this couple, who never even visited America, would feel at home on a campus that values both faith and family.

The trees on the University of Dayton's sprawling campus often hold hidden and deeply personal meaning. Some of us can't walk under their foliage without stealing a moment to reminisce, to pray silently.

We know more than 1,545 magnolia, white ash, pine and other trees border pathways and stand like sentinels on the campus lawns and in nearby neighborhoods. Our scientists can calculate the reduction of the university's carbon footprint every time a tree is planted.

Yet neither is the true measure of a single tree.

Friends of James "Gerbs" Grabowski donated a swamp white oak that was planted near the gazebo in view of the iconic Hail Mary statue. Gerbs proposed to his wife, Tracey, at the gazebo in 1991. For generations to come, this mighty oak will shade other young lovers. A young friend of the family promises to "high five" the tree every time he passes it on his way to the library.

The family of humorist Erma Bombeck, a member of the Class of 1949, chose a hardy Hoopsii blue spruce to plant near her Ohio historical marker outside St. Mary Hall. "They planted trees and crabgrass came up," the plaque reads. What better tribute to a delightfully funny writer whose newspaper columns chronicling suburban family life hung on the refrigerator doors of our youth?

During Reunion Weekend in June, the family of Congressman Chuck Whalen will bless a dawn redwood tree in front of Roesch Library, which houses a collection of Whalen's congressional and personal papers.

I know exactly how these families feel about these trees.

Each spring, when the crimson leaves on the Japanese maple make their regal appearance, their beauty will remind me what a tree is worth.

You can't put a price on it.

(Spring 2012)

For Sale

It's an inexplicable feeling to see a "For Sale" sign on the lawn of the only house I grew up in.

I moved out decades ago, but my childhood memories will always reside at 112 Inverness Ave. in this quirky ranch house. A raft of emotions washed over me as I pulled in the driveway for a final visit before a young family would claim this address as their own.

No childhood is idyllic, except perhaps through the distorted lens of time. Yet, we grew up in a more innocent age in a working-class neighborhood overflowing with kids — your own social set of ready-made friends. All of us had the same type of 1950s-era, no-frills starter home in the shadow of a GM plant. We thought this was the way all people lived.

How six of us shared a house with one shower remains one of the mysteries of my youth. We negotiated the bath schedule every night while arguing over whose turn it was to do the supper dishes in a kitchen that barely provided enough space to carve a Christmas turkey. My sister Nancy and I shared a bedroom, where we slept on matching twin beds. On my side of the bedroom, I hung posters of Bobby Sherman and other teen heartthrobs from *Tiger Beat* magazine. To this day, we can't imagine how we equally divided a closet and dresser without a brawl over who deserved an extra drawer.

As we outgrew the house, my parents built a big wood-paneled room on the back, a construction project that required putting another door through our bedroom. As my brothers ambled through our room anytime they pleased, Nancy and I lost all semblance of privacy.

Yet we all gained a spacious family room, half-bath and dining area that would accommodate our growing extended family for holiday gatherings. Alas, while the addition nearly doubled the size of the house to what, by neighborhood standards, seemed an almost-extravagant 1,766 square feet, it did not include what we yearned for the most — another shower.

That was OK, though, since we never spent much time in the house. A neighborhood filled with friends beckoned us outdoors, and we would disappear for hours on end until my mother yelled out the door for 5 p.m. dinner. Who eats dinner that early anymore?

The nightly summer game of hide-and-seek at dusk had rules so elaborate ("You can't go into that yard EVER, no stepping on those flowers, no hiding here or there") that it's a wonder the game ever felt as spontaneous and fun as it did.

We played pickup baseball games at the tiny park across the street, where you learned how to field a ball that would carom wildly off the water tower in the middle of the outfield. That's a life skill.

In the winters, we skated on a tiny patch of ice in a neighbor's yard. In our tennis shoes.

I had to walk only a few steps outside the front door to babysitting jobs. Fighting nerves, I remember backing out of that driveway to make my first journey to Ohio University to enter journalism school, questioning if I had what it took — and wondering if I'd ever come back. Until my father's death, I never missed a Christmas in that house.

To everything there is a season. It was time to close the door for the last time, knowing this house would always be home.

Walking back to the car, I realized you can never put a "For Sale" sign on memories.

The Art of Letting Go

"The blackberries gleam like glass, like the glass ornaments we hang on trees in December to remind ourselves to be grateful for snow."

After one of my childhood best friends died on the Fourth of July, my friend Scott reached out to share a poignant Margaret Atwood poem, "Blackberries," about savoring life's sweetness before it's gone.

For months Holly lay helpless in a Reno, Nevada, hospital bed, kept alive by a ventilator, a tracheotomy and hope. She could only mouth words and, for a stretch, her longtime partner, Norbert, said she silently talked up a storm to him. In a FaceTime call a week before she died, she nodded her head several times as I regaled her with stories of our youthful escapades. When she tried to respond, I couldn't hear her, but I understood three words: "I love you." Earlier that week, she scribbled three words to Norbert: "Help me die."

Six words, sparse yet undeniable. "The hardest thing to say sometimes is, 'I want what you want,'" said my son Ali, a mental health counselor.

It was time for us to let go.

Outside my home office window this summer, the cicadas emerged from a 17-year hiatus to create quite a ruckus for a few weeks before mating and dying. At first, their shrill singsong annoyed me, but as Holly's life slipped away, I listened anew to their poetic call. Isn't life all about love and loss?

Holly and I became inseparable friends in high school when

we played on the softball team and in summer leagues. During those vulnerable coming-of-age years, we spent hours playing ball, hitting the tennis courts, drinking Little Kings and hanging out on muggy Ohio summer evenings, the night sky twinkling with fireflies. We never thought their light would dim, let alone ours.

After we embarked to universities on the opposite ends of the state, we faithfully stayed in touch through lengthy letters — half news, half philosophical musings — that I still store in a shoebox. One summer break we set out in my rusted '69 Oldsmobile 442 on a zany mission to meet my teen idol Gary Puckett at Americana Amusement Park, where we managed to talk our way backstage. Flash forward to another summer, when she joined my sister Nancy and my college roommates as bridesmaids at my wedding. A candid photo captured her smiling face as the women laughed and teased the bemused groom.

And now, this summer.

Shortly after midnight on Independence Day, Holly found freedom from a body battered by cancer and a host of insurmountable health challenges. As fireworks lit up the Lake Michigan sky near our summer home, my husband, Zafar, unfolded a sky lantern. I swear I bought only brightly colored ones, so how did a white memorial lantern end up on the top of the stack? It was inscribed with the words, "May this light rise to the heavens to shine with you through all eternity." Astonished, we stared at the lantern in reverent silence as our neighbor Kate picked up a pen and scrawled Holly's name on it.

As Zafar lit the mini hot air balloon and gently guided it upward over the tranquil waves, Ali said softly, "That's a God moment." When I texted a photo to my friend Anna, she replied, "It gave me chills of recognition of so many things we rarely get to glimpse. It's beyond poignant and honestly kind of magical."

Standing on the sand, I watched the floating lantern become a tiny, then indistinguishable, dot in the inky sky. I knew its light couldn't last forever — just like the sweetness of summer's blackberries or the fleeting love call of cicadas.

Yet, in my sadness, I gratefully embraced this moment as one of life's unexpected gifts, a reminder of the soaring power of love.

(Summer 2021)

WORK-LIFE
BALANCE

I Quit

A funny thing happened on the way to quitting my job.

I discovered that on any given day, a lot of my colleagues and friends could imagine impulsively throwing in the towel, too.

It's not that we don't enjoy our jobs; mine has kept me fulfilled for a decade. It's simply that we've lost balance.

One day you wake up feeling exhausted, with a to-do list longer than a grocery list. You feel as though you're perched precariously in the air on a teeter-totter with a growing assortment of responsibilities weighing down the other side: young children, a neglected husband, aging parents, looming deadlines, baskets of laundry. And you realize you're about to turn 40 and you don't have time to reflect on this pivotal point in your life: middle age. You're too overwhelmed being a mother, a wife, a daughter, a boss, a colleague and a friend to find equilibrium, to reassess life at the halfway point.

So, I impetuously quit my job.

I wanted to be a modern-day Henry David Thoreau, to drop out of civilization to sojourn in solitude in the wilderness. A teething toddler still in diapers dispelled that notion quicker than the sudden, jarring pop of a balloon that meanders too close to the fireplace. But I could take control of my life, "to stand on the meeting of two eternities, the past and the future, which is precisely the present moment; to toe that line," as Thoreau so eloquently wrote in *Walden*.

Thoreau went to the woods for two years; I dropped out for six weeks. My resignation turned into a long vacation and an eventual return to the job I'd left, but I went back with a new perspective that only an expanse of time can provide — along with a supportive boss, who gave me greater flexibility and, more importantly, permission. "You give everyone on your staff a break, except yourself," she said.

During my six-week hiatus, my husband and I left the children with a friend and spent four perfect days on a beach — our first trip alone together in eight years. I chauffeured the 7-year-old to school and basketball practices and games and savored spare time on the living room floor with our 18-month-old. Although we own more than 100 children's books, we read *Go, Dog, Go!* and *Brown Bear, Brown Bear, What Do You See?* dozens of times. I mixed up the childhood standards with the Beach Boys' "Barbara Ann," much to my toddler's merriment. We talked about the differences between animals, that they're not all dogs or ducks. He ignored me: When we went to a friend's house for dinner and to the nursing home to visit my grandmother, he labeled both cats he met as dogs. Well, it was clear to him that they weren't ducks.

He did learn where his nose is.

On most days, we wandered over to my childhood home, where I cooked dinner for my parents. Until I had children and learned that managing their upbringing is far more difficult than managing an office, I distanced myself from my homemaker mother. Now, as she struggled to recover from the aftermath of a heart attack and stroke, I felt grateful for the moments that we could spend together, and I continued to marvel at how she once managed to take a shower and cook dinner with four children under age 5 underfoot. Suddenly, I took extraordinary pleasure in folding her laundry and attempting to recreate the simple suppers she fixed for a brood that took sustenance for granted.

My husband's words echo in my ears: "Money comes and

goes, but what's really important is your family. You have to take care of your family."

As our youngest finds joy in finding his nose and learning other simple life lessons, I've had the opportunity to slow down, to appreciate the present moment, to take stock. With that comes the realization that, as a member of the fabled Sandwich Generation, I will continue to feel overwhelmed as I try to balance a full life with a fulfilling career.

But maybe that's what's meant to be. Maybe that's what middle age is all about. It's carrying a mental to-do list that spans the conference table and the dining room table. It's cutting up meat for your children — and your mother.

It's the ability to appreciate the extraordinary in ordinary moments.

It's not about quitting.

(Spring 1998)

A Living. A Life.

"I'm pregnant!"

When you're making an important announcement, a quip can defuse the tension.

After my colleagues laughed loudly, I shared the real news: I was leaving my job to devote more energy to writing and special projects — in a part-time role with the university's president, in an effort to find that elusive work-life balance. I soon lost count of the number of people who expressed their envy.

Before longtime University of Dayton President Brother Ray Fitz took a chance and promoted a 29-year-old newcomer to lead the PR office, he asked me, "Can you make a commitment?"

In a quarter of a century, I had the opportunity to help shape the public image of two outstanding presidents, hire gifted creative people, interview the biggest names in school history and announce virtually every major campus story. I'm humbled by the experience and deeply grateful for the trust bestowed on me.

It's been the best job anyone could ever hope to hold. Still, I will not miss middle-of-the-night phone calls about what one of my favorite administrators euphemistically called "special events" — a little havoc in the student neighborhood.

It's time to write the next chapter.

Or maybe it's time to pause, reflect and rewrite the definition of "work."

Here's what I learned since quitting my job.

No. 1: We long for balance in our lives. I received hundreds of emails and Facebook comments, and that theme pervades. We all want more time in our lives — for our family, for our friends, for our passions. "I know so many people who are just drained," said one journalist friend with twin sons.

No. 2: This yearning doesn't come from just my stressed-out women friends. Men, too, seek greater balance. "(I'm still) figuring out the rat race's exit ramp," wrote a younger male friend.

No. 3: Work is life. A friend pointed me to an essay by Carolyn Woo, president and CEO of Catholic Relief Services. "There is so much of me that has grown through work. It is the place where I put my values to the test. ... Was I worthy of the trust put in me? Did I pause to let grace have a chance?" she wrote for the Catholic News Service.

No. 4: Our lives are a calling. Before I decided to quit, I sat quietly, closed my eyes and listened to the beating heart of my passion. I let it rush over me like waves at a seashore, drowning out the nagging voice of doubt and insecurity. Then I followed my heart.

Unlike many friends downsized out of jobs in their later years, I asked for the chance to rightsize my life in a new, part-time gig that allows me time to unplug.

"Can you make a commitment?" a university president once asked me. Today, I realize why it's still so easy to say with confidence, "Yes."

I'm saying it to myself this time.

(Winter 2014)

And Why Not?

"Happy birthday month, girlfriend! Lunch sometime during the celebration window?" I wrote on Sharon's Facebook wall.

Between bites of salad at our usual spot, I teased her about scheduling birthday meals with friends practically every day of the week throughout August.

"And why not?" she asked with a laugh.

As young professionals, we worked overtime climbing the corporate ladder, trying to prove that we were just as effective leaders as men. We held impressive titles, stubbornly clung to the myth that we could "have it all" and, too often, worked through lunch.

Not these days. We're letting go and discovering a deeper sense of fulfillment.

I'm slowly working my way down the ladder after a career as the longest-serving communications director in the University of Dayton's history. Sharon left a stressful management position in television news and now handles public relations for a local hospital system. As she nears retirement, she says half-jokingly, "I'm not climbing over anyone. I'm climbing home."

We're not the only women reevaluating the work-life conundrum and reexamining the idea of "having it all." I don't have to look any farther than a recent issue of *Millie*, a women's personal finance magazine, to see how women are addressing these matters on our own terms. A bold headline, "The Big Pivot: Real Women on How They Redefined Their Work and Their Lives," leapt off the cover. Inside, women relayed their stories of creating lives of greater purpose and happiness.

"One day I was at our big resort in Palm Springs and looked out the window and thought, 'I don't want to be here anymore,'" said a national account manager for Marriott who quit and founded a vacation-house management company on Georgia's Tybee Island. A former senior executive producer for public television in Minnesota now works as a seasonal park ranger in Alaska, where she produces live educational broadcasts for millions of people who view, of all things, bear cams. "It is thrilling, invigorating and healing to be with the bears all the time," she told the magazine. She relishes walking home "with bears and birds and the peace of the wilderness."

My friends are mastering reinvention, too. Nancy, a clinical psychologist in Pittsburgh, left a full-time, tenure-track position in academia to learn podcasting and flex her creative muscle as a writer. Today, she interviews Deepak Chopra, Dolly Parton and other celebrities for her podcast and writes stories about their journeys for national publications. She's managed to knock out two books, too.

"I think when a creative dream keeps nagging you, sometimes you start paying attention. You can dream about doing it all, but most of us have to make a choice," she said. "Looking back, it really did mean shifting the definition of success."

Nancy and I have a mutual friend who could offer a master class in redefining accomplishment. As the first female CEO of a New York ad agency and a classic Type A overachiever, Mary Lou was working "a gazillion hours" when she decided to briefly step away and recalibrate.

"Five weeks (away) is a lifetime when you are CEO. I just hung out in my neighborhood, met my friends and de-caffed myself.

It was a wonderful pause button in my life and a life-changing time because in daring to go cold turkey from the office and live in my life, I started to gain a sense of self-awareness and identify what was important to me and how I wanted to move forward," she said.

Mary Lou wound up leaving the corner office to launch a marketing agency. Offers rolled in to co-host a reality TV show, give motivational talks and pen columns for national magazines. When her mother died, she worked through her grief by writing *The God Box*, a keepsake book about the handwritten notes and prayers her mother tucked away in little boxes as a way of letting go of her worries. After the book landed on *The New York Times'* bestseller list, Mary Lou turned it into a one-woman touring show. As an actress and producer, she's now staged more than 100 solo performances, which have raised over $500,000 for charity.

My own reinvention is not nearly as dramatic, but it has filled my heart with new purpose. When I told University of Dayton President Dan Curran that I was burned out and wanted to retire when I turned 55, he wanted to know about my plans. "I want to read books and walk on the beach," I said. "OK, after that, then what?" he asked. "I want to write more."

Guided by those ideas, we fashioned a part-time job that gave me time to read the neglected books on my nightstand and mix writing a president's speeches with more of my own work. With a lighter schedule, I could devote energy to building the Erma Bombeck Writers' Workshop, which brings equal doses of inspiration and joy to my life. I finally quit procrastinating and compiled my writings for a book.

Without guilt, I now take luxuriously long lunches with friends and even longer weekends walking along a Lake Michigan shoreline, the seagulls soaring in the distance. I've made peace with stepping away at the top of my game to chase my dreams.

And why not?

(Winter 2021)

A WRITER'S
JOURNEY

Onward and Upward, Erma Nation

One writer likened the virtual Erma Bombeck Writers' Workshop to "a working cruise ship sans the pool and deck."

Another felt "LOL aftershocks," and one quipped that she did not want the virtual belly laughs to subside. "Are they going to make us leave when this ends? I'm not leaving. I'm not moving from here until the next Erma Bombeckalooza or maybe not forever," she said.

When a global pandemic forced me to reschedule the spring workshop for the fall and then swallow my apprehension and take the event online, I did not envision nearly 700 writers from around the world, in the zany spirit of the conference, camped out at their laptops, more than a few in pajamas, bathrobes, Halloween masks and the occasional tiara.

Wearing an aged robe with a surgical mask looped over her ear, longtime emcee Patricia Wynn Brown, a professional performer with pitch-perfect comedic timing, set the tone in an opening monologue from her basement laundry room in Columbus, Ohio.

"Right now we can use a boost. We can take a page from *Aunt Erma's Cope Book*. WWEW — What would Erma want? She'd want us to buck up, slip on our muumuus, put on our Sansabelt pants, throw in a load, sit in our easy chair and drink our favorite beverage," said the unflappable Brown. "Onward and upward, Erma Nation."

Humor saves us, and we had gathered across time zones to be restored. "We're taking a small, but needed, detour from this moment in the world to do some mining of comedy and refreshing of the human spirit," reflected *New York Times* bestselling author Annabelle Gurwitch from her Los Angeles study. Earlier, Mike Rowe of *Dirty Jobs* fame deadpanned, "I don't fully understand what goes on at this bacchanalia, but I like it."

As the virtual workshop came to life on my computer screen, I realized I had underestimated the hunger of writers for connection and the power of laughter to heal. "We are conjuring the magic of hope, renewal, inspiration and joy," Brown observed.

At times, the weekend felt like a group therapy session after a year of quarantines, travel curtailment, a worsening pandemic and the greatest civil unrest since the 1960s. We needed this ready-made support system.

The online chat bar sped by like a freight train with colorful comments and wisecracks. Writers on the West Coast set their alarms to catch the 6 a.m. sessions live instead of watching the recordings later. "I haven't run to the refrigerator once, the true mark of audience engagement," noted syndicated columnist Suzette Martinez Standring. One thread wove throughout this gathering of witty wordsmiths: Can we find words of humor and hope for healing not just ourselves, but a broken world?

"Your writing is your higher calling. It is the thing you must be doing when the world seems to be falling apart because that may be the thing that helps the world stay together in ways you can't even imagine," said novelist and essayist Sophfronia Scott in a poignant keynote rallying cry.

"What if this is your opportunity to speak comfort to someone with the same sense of one-on-one intimacy that you and I have right now?" she asked. "The Nobel Prize-winning author Toni Morrison said, 'This is *precisely* the time when artists go to work. There is no time for despair, no place for self-pity, no need for silence, no room for fear. We speak, we write, we do language.

That is how civilizations heal.'"

As Scott's words hung in the air, I heard the echo of humor icon Erma Bombeck. "When humor goes," she wrote, "there goes civilization."

Humor saves us. It connects us. Its heart beats with hope.

"To connect is the highest aspiration for humans," Gurwitch told writers. "I think that's what great writing does, whether it's writing on the page or writing on the stage in the form of a joke. It compresses the space between our lives."

Even when life is no laughing matter, "the world needs you to write your heart out," urged keynoter and stand-up comic Wendy Liebman. "Write, Ermas, write — and do not waste time."

(Autumn 2020)

Inevitable Flow

With hesitance and the look of a writer lost in thought, she glanced at me between bites of a caramel-frosted pastry and sips of coffee.

As I started to speak, 81-year-old Helena Borgmann picked up her cup, still half-full, and walked slowly across the roomful of writers' workshop participants at Sinclair Community College. Her baggy hose and flowered hat put her somewhat oddly out of place with this different generation of hopeful writers.

How many half-cups of coffee got cold as she worked a phrase over in her mind, searching for that elusive right word? I wondered.

I drank coffee and chatted that weekend with John Jakes, author of the American Bicentennial novels. I listened to literary great John Gardner and Jakes talk with enthusiasm about communicating simply, directly and vividly through the written word.

But it was this tiny, slightly bent-over, elderly woman who showed me what striving to feel fulfilled as a writer really means.

"It just doesn't come easy, you know," she said as I sat down beside her in Blair Hall auditorium for the opening remarks.

As I nodded, she pulled out, with trembling fingers, a stapled copy of *Jewels in the Sun*, one of four poetry books she's penned in the last decade.

"I looked on the river — And thought of life's currents. Now, fast, now slow, inevitable — And then I became tranquil again." I slowly read and reread one of the book's 96 poems.

Simple. Direct. Vivid.

I learned that although she didn't graduate from high school, she enjoys free college courses offered for senior citizens at the downtown Dayton community college. *Golden Sheaves* will be her last poetry book because she can no longer afford 50 cents for postage and a dime for a manila envelope to send her works off to some little-known publisher.

"Will you continue to write poems about nature?" I asked.

She blinked in confusion. *What an absurd question*, I suddenly thought.

"If you don't do anything, you think of all kinds of things," she responded, staring intently ahead. "When am I going to die? How long am I going to live?"

Asked to retire 11 years ago from her job as a secretary and German translator at Wright-Patterson Air Force Base, Borgmann didn't sit around all afternoon wondering what to fix for dinner. Instead, she picked up a pen and returned to her first love of writing.

Something John Gardner had told me seemed to offer reassurance Borgmann might need to hear, so later in the day, I looked for her, my notepad open to Gardner's words: "The person who sits and believes in the thing he's doing is going to make the work of art. Any way of presenting language is yours and authentically yours."

I wanted to share those words with the spry poet I'd met earlier.

But I could not find her flowered hat in the workshop crowd. She must have already left for her afternoon political science class.

(Spring 1979)

Humor Writing's Hottest Ticket

Raj Jaiswal twice missed out on registering for the University of Dayton's Erma Bombeck Writers' Workshop after it sold out within hours in 2014 and 2016. After that, it turned into a bit of an obsession.

"It became my forbidden fruit," confessed Jaiswal, an emergency room doctor in New York City who has written comedy sketches, including a sitcom script.

En route to Mumbai, India, when registration opened in 2018, he checked on the availability of Wi-Fi on the plane, but he turned it down because of the expense.

"When I landed in Mumbai, I was still fuming from my decision not to pay for the in-flight Wi-Fi and lamenting my middle-class upbringing," he said. "As I checked my phone, I realized that I had spectacularly miscalculated the time difference. Instantly, all my anger converted to shame and embarrassment.

"I'm Indian; we are supposed to be good at numbers, and I got this wrong," he joked, adding tongue-in-cheek, "I felt the disapproving shame of a billion people while waiting to collect my luggage. I felt so sad that I had not lived up to the cultural stereotype, something I have aspired to do all my life. The only saving grace from all of this was that at least I still had some time."

He scurried to his hotel, checked in and logged on to the registration site on his international phone — only to discover the internet connection was painfully slow. It timed out after he partially filled out the form.

"I wasn't sure if I had registered 11 times or if it had even gone through," Jaiswal said. Though this was not a "typical 2 a.m. crisis," he told the desk clerk he was desperate. "There I was using a random stranger's phone, putting in all my credit card details" in the middle of the night for a workshop 8,000 miles away.

But he got in.

Was it worth it?

"I don't know if the world should be subjected to my writing, but the workshop invigorated my writing spirit," said Jaiswal, who impressed fellow attendees with his on-the-spot humorous writing about a Parisian dance contest in Kathy Kinney and Cindy Ratzlaff's "How to Uncover Your Own Voice" workshop.

Jaiswal discovered the spirit of Erma Nation—the reason the 2018 gathering sold out in a record four hours and 42 minutes. It's unlike any other writers' workshop in the country. Emcee Patricia Wynn Brown, who once tagged the workshop the "Woodstock of Humor," offered this amusing take after the spring workshop garnered the highest ratings in its history: "It's *Pee-Wee's Playhouse* and a bit of *David Letterman*—in the Bombeck kitchen."

Stand-up comic Leighann Lord, who's served as keynoter and faculty member, lovingly called the workshop "our communal and biennial home."

Every other spring, authors, bloggers, essayists and humorists make the pilgrimage to Erma's alma mater to honor her legacy, laugh and soak in advice, tips and encouragement from other writers. They mingle with the Bombeck family and keynoters like Liza Donnelly, the brilliant *New Yorker* and CBS News cartoonist; John Grogan, author of the bestseller *Marley & Me;* and the hysterically funny Monica Piper, Emmy Award-winning comedy writer for the animated series *Rugrats*.

Beyond the laughter that reverberates for three days, the workshop has a serious mission — to inspire writers in the same way

Erma felt buoyed by her English professor's three simple words of encouragement: "You can write!"

Author and performer David Henry Sterry and his agent-wife Arielle Eckstut have brought their popular "Pitchapalooza," described as "*American Idol* for books, only gentler," to the workshop several times in an unusual return-after-return engagement.

The explanation is simple, Sterry said.

"This is the most supportive, generous, loving place writers can gather."

(Spring 2018)

A High Calling

"John Jakes knows more facts than any historian I know and treats them with a lighter heart. Out of it comes an artistic vision. ... It's John Jakes as if he were God running history."

— John Gardner

At first glance John Jakes looks like the stereotypical high school history teacher who would rather be conducting football practice than writing Civil War battle dates on the blackboard.

The tall, heavyset Jakes, with a thick thatch of gray hair, is neither a history teacher nor a football coach. But he hardly looks like a historical novelist, either.

Contracted by Pyramid Books to write The Kent Family Chronicles, an eight-book series for the U.S. bicentennial, Jakes pounded out nearly every word on a $35, secondhand "wonderful little Underwood" in his basement in Kettering, Ohio.

"I'm no historian or social thinker," the writer readily conceded in a chat over coffee at a writers' workshop at Sinclair Community College in Dayton, Ohio. "There's an immense range of stylistic talent displayed by people who write unreadable books. People who write history," he observed, "don't begin to give you the color and excitement (of the times). I always think of historians (as those) sitting around talking about lofty theories of history."

History textbooks don't tell readers, as Jakes does in the yet-to-be-published *The Americans,* that newspaper magnate William Randolph Hearst kept an alligator in his closet. In true *Harvard Lampoon* spirit, Hearst occasionally got the gator drunk.

In one sequence in *The Furies*, Jakes richly re-creates the hysteria of California gold rush fever. Stove lids and furniture sank in the mud as the get-rich-quick pioneers anxiously raced west, discarding weighty personal belongings along the way.

Jakes' novelistic flair fits the bill of literary writer John Gardner's definition of a gifted writer — one who creates a vivid and continuous dream in the reader's mind.

"It's when you pick up a book after breakfast and then someone taps you on the shoulder and says, 'You've missed lunch. Are you going to have supper?'" observed Gardner at the writers' workshop. "It seems to me John Jakes fulfills it."

In the same down-to-earth appeal apparent in his writings, Jakes shrugs off that praise. "I don't consider myself literary anything," he said. "There's no way you can go out and court continuing success. You write what you feel; you write what you are."

The American Bicentennial novels, he said, strongly reflect a wide range of personal feelings about America, love, family, bigotry and justice. Through his writing, he seeks to reassure readers of their resiliency.

"We forget the devastation of the Civil War," he noted, adding, "I think people are looking to history for reassurance that we have come through tough times (intact)."

Jakes describes his readers as a tapestry of Americans from "corporate executives to convicts in the pen," and they are following the Kent family through history, either through the written power of his books or the television adaptations. The $3.6 million Universal production of *The Bastard* has already aired twice with plans for *The Rebels* and *The Seekers* to follow.

With 27 million copies of the first seven books on the market and the anticipated release of *The Americans*, Jakes has come a long way from his early days as a struggling, self-described "imitation Ray Bradbury" science fiction writer — one who sold his first story in 1951.

When publisher Donald A. Wollheim said Jakes' name was not suitably romantic for a historical novel, Jakes used the pseudonym Jay Scotland for six historical novels set in medieval times. They didn't sell well, but he kept writing. Before *The Bastard*, the first book in the American Bicentennial series, and between copywriting for advertising agencies, Jakes wrote 52 books and 200 short stories, mostly science fiction. "There are a few faithful readers," Jakes said, tongue firmly in cheek.

Still, he's yet to travel as far as he had intended through U.S. history. Originally hoping to bring the Kent family through 200 years of American history, he winds up at the end of the 19th century.

"I did start with a basic plan, but that quickly went out the window. Characters do that wonderful thing of taking over the story. The trap I fell into," he said half-apologetically, "was becoming too enamored with the personalities of history."

Jakes spent four months researching each book, mostly in the downtown Dayton, Ohio, library, before spending another four months behind the typewriter. And for now, he says eight books are enough.

"It's like a play that goes on and on and on for the sake of going on," he said. "I'd much rather drop the series at a point before people say, 'Why didn't he quit?'"

Still, Jakes knows he doesn't always know when to quit.

"I was slow to learn," he told the creative writing workshop audience. "It took me two years in high school to learn you can't send (a manuscript) in (to a publisher) written in longhand on two sides of notebook paper," he said.

Although he's always desired to be a playwright, Jakes said he'll probably continue to write historical novels.

"The real secret (to writing) is persistence. I've always fancied myself to be a writer of limited ability," he said with characteristic humility.

Away from his Hilton Head, South Carolina, beach home to be in Dayton for a few days last month, Jakes didn't let the trip sidetrack him from work. He brought the final draft of *The Americans* to polish during free hours.

"It's a religion. It's a high calling," he said.

(Spring 1979)

Part Love Letter,
Part Family Reunion, Part Pep Talk

For three days, we laughed.

OK, we howled. So much so that we dubbed the University of Dayton's biennial Erma Bombeck Writers' Workshop the "Woodstock of Humor."

But it's not just the sound of laughter I remember from the gathering of 350 writers from around the nation.

My eyes closed, I listened to Suzette Martinez Standring's gentle, melodic voice guiding a group of writers through a creative-writing exercise. A trained hypnotherapist and author, she urged us to tap deep into our subconscious, to use our mind like a "3D coloring book" to create our own Instagram out of a long-ago memory.

I flashed back to January 1988 and a quick break during a University of Dayton board of trustees meeting. I am early in my university career, and I worry about getting this video assignment right.

Erma Bombeck, then a trustee at her alma mater, sits in front of me and delivers an 84-second anecdote about how Brother Tom Price, her English professor, first told her she had a gift for writing. She speaks directly from the heart to the videographer as though we are all dear friends. No notes. No hesitation. No pretense.

Her words still give me a chill.

"So I must tell you, you sort of slide things under the door and wait until the great critic comments on them," she recalls. "And he saw me one day outside the cafeteria, and he said three words to me, that's all, just three words that were to sustain me for the rest of my life, I think. He looked at me and said, 'You can write.'"

I can't suppress a laugh when she quips, "I won't believe him. And then I thought, 'No, he's a man of the cloth.' I mean he'd have to be on his knees for the rest of his life repenting for this if he didn't mean it."

Her words, filled with warmth and humility, spoke to this young writer. Years later, working with the Bombeck family and a group of alumni, I launched the Erma Bombeck Writers' Workshop, a labor of love that we run on a shoestring.

The 2012 workshop sold out in eight days, without any slick marketing. Jill Fales, a columnist for the *Orange County Register*, sat patiently by her computer and waited for online registration to open. "It was like getting concert tickets to the Rolling Stones," said the first-time workshop attendee.

Writers know this workshop is different. It's part love letter, part family reunion, part pep talk. Authors, mommy bloggers and humorists all make the pilgrimage to Dayton, Ohio, to honor Erma's legacy and soak in advice, tips and encouragement from other writers. They mingle and laugh with the Bombeck family and celebrity writers such as Alan Zweibel, one of the original *Saturday Night Live* writers, and the hysterically funny Adriana Trigiani, who has created lively novels like *Big Stone Gap*.

To those who grew up with Erma's columns hanging on their refrigerator doors, Erma always felt like our next-door neighbor. Her writing captured the foibles of family life in a way that made us laugh at ourselves. "My idea of housework," she once wrote, "is to sweep the room with a glance."

We've tried to bottle Erma's spirit.

"I don't know of any other writers' conference where the

famous and the unknown sit side by side in mutual respect. That's Erma," observed Tracy Beckerman, a nationally syndicated humor columnist and author from New Jersey who found the confidence to write after attending her first Bombeck workshop in 2006. Today, she's on the workshop's faculty.

"When I came to my first conference, I had one column in one small-town newspaper. The support of this writing community is incredible," she said.

Writers leave the workshop renewed and inspired, ready to find their own voice.

"People may tell you you're the next Erma Bombeck. No, you're not," author and stand-up comic Nancy Berk cautioned writers in her session on summoning "The Power of Erma."

"Do it your way. Listen to the voices that matter."

Just like Erma did.

(Summer 2012)

A Special Gift

A treasured gift — a clock with a smiling photo of Bill and Erma Bombeck — sits on my cluttered office desk.

"The clock photo thing was a part of her office. The picture had been changed. (She probably had Paul what's-his-name Newman in it)," wrote Bill Bombeck in a funny, touching thank-you note after the Erma Bombeck Conference on Popular American Humor at the University of Dayton. "The success was beyond my wildest dreams."

The scrawled note and gift illustrate how, even after her death, beloved humorist Erma Bombeck brings people together. For four days, we laughed. But we were also deeply moved by the Bombeck family's willingness to share the personal — from their memories to 41 banker's boxes full of manuscripts, columns, correspondence and other evidence of a full, creative life.

Her children listened to scholars analyze their mother's work, more often shared as clippings in women's letters to friends than as footnotes in scholarly papers. Andy Bombeck, a schoolteacher, conceded that it was "a little weird" but intriguing to listen to college professors talk about his mother's gift of humor. When he was growing up, Matt Bombeck, now a television writer, had no idea what his mother did for a living. "We told everybody that she was a syndicated communist."

At a luncheon presentation of the Bombeck papers, a replay of Phil Donahue's touching eulogy brought fresh tears to the eyes of Erma's daughter, Betsy, even four years after her mother's death. "We shall never see the likes of her again. She was real and brought us down to earth — gently, generously and with brilliant humor," Donahue said. "When the scholars gather hundreds of years from now to learn about us, they can't know it all if they don't read Erma."

Any trace of tears quickly evaporated into peals of laughter. "The reason we're here is that Bill Bombeck finally got around to cleaning out Erma's desk," quipped neighbor and *Family Circus* cartoonist Bil Keane. "When I die, my wife is going to donate my papers to Goodwill."

As I think back over those few extraordinary days, I remember the one-liners. Feisty Liz Carpenter's description of herself and Erma: "the Thelma and Louise of the ERA movement." Art Buchwald's one-word deadpan, "sex," when asked why he and Erma became such close friends.

But I always come back to the one-liner Erma heard as a student at the University of Dayton, when Brother Tom Price gave her confidence with the three magical words every young, insecure writer yearns to hear: "You can write."

In his letter, Bill Bombeck described the clock as "a remembrance from Erma (and Bill) on the anniversary of her passing."

For me, this clock will always symbolize a moment in time when Erma's family, her friends and other gifted writers came together to remember, to laugh, to honor a woman who took those three magical words to heart.

(Summer 2000)

'Kid, You've Got a Great Future'

Sorting through old letters a couple months ago, I stumbled across a 1979 congratulatory telegram from Erma Bombeck, of all people.

I had just won a $500 Marj Heyduck Scholarship and welcomed the unexpected cash for journalism school tuition. Today, just days after coming down from the high of the 2010 Erma Bombeck Writers' Workshop at the University of Dayton, Erma's encouraging words unexpectedly greet me again.

"I would love to pull you aside and sit in a corner somewhere and share with you the legend who bears the name of the scholarship you have just received," she wrote. "I knew Marj Heyduck for over 20 years. As a copy girl at age 15 she was the first to see in me that hungry look that says 'I want to write.' She saw me off to college, hired me when I returned, bought gifts for my babies and resisted the urge to use a black pencil on my copy and allowed me to be myself."

Be yourself.

From *New York Times* columnist Gail Collins to *Fox & Friends* morning host Steve Doocy, workshop presenters urged writers to find their voice by looking in their heart. "From Erma I learned that if you write about things simply and honestly, they come up miraculously funny," Collins said. "Have a little heart — that's the secret," shared Doocy, recounting a hilarious bonding moment with his daughters during an outing for pedicures.

As if there were some doubt about Erma's enduring legacy as a writer, screenwriter son Matt Bombeck removed it, repeating:

"Your writing has to have heart. Your writing has to have honesty. People knew that about her."

Tracy Beckerman, a delightfully engaging and funny blogger mom from New Jersey, may be the modern-day Erma. "I came to my first workshop in 2006. I knew nothing about nothing, but I left here so juiced," she remembered. By the time she returned to the 2008 workshop, she had syndicated her *Lost in Suburbia* column in 50 newspapers. Today, her column appears in 400 newspapers nationally, reaching 3.5 million readers in 25 states, and she's written a book, *Rebel Without a Minivan*.

Like Erma, she knows her audience. "See all those young men in the Marriott bar last night?" she asked a room full of mostly women writers who gathered to hear how they can syndicate their work. "They were out to see some cougars. On one side, we have hot men. The other side, we're having hot flashes."

Mo Rocca and a crew from *CBS Sunday Morning* hung out for three days to talk to Tracy and other writers and interview Erma's children about the humorist's legacy, nowhere more prevalent than at her hometown alma mater for three laugh-filled days in April. Hustling between sessions, first-time workshop director Matt Dewald used the phrase "magic in a bottle" to describe the workshop's spirit.

For Matt and our colleagues, this workshop is a labor of love. It's not our day job. We write brochure copy, ads, the occasional magazine feature. We pitch news stories, update websites. I sit in planning meetings and think about writing that book every writer has in the back of her head. Every two years, Erma reminds us of the magic of our words, the sheer joy of writing.

Decades later she's still reminding me — and all the writers we've touched at the workshop we run in her honor — that you can't ever take yourself too seriously.

I laughed, reading the forgotten closing of that long-ago telegram.

"May I add my best wishes and as Marj said when I returned from the Ohio Newspaper Women's Association competition winning only a beer cooler as a door prize, 'Kid, you've got a great future.'"

(Spring 2010)

'Get Out and Look at the World'

A writer can't put words to paper without taking time to observe life up close, storyteller and humorist Garrison Keillor told more than 300 writers from around the country in a keynote speech kicking off the University of Dayton's 2008 Erma Bombeck Writers' Workshop.

"My advice to writers is very simple. It is to get out," he said. "It is to get out for long walks. Writing is an obsessive activity. Walk for 2 or 3 miles every day — rapidly if necessary — and get out and look at the world. When writing loses touch with the beautiful surface of the world, it loses its way."

With the Bombeck family in the audience, Keillor devoted a good portion of his talk to Erma Bombeck's legacy.

"She was a great writer, a writer always true to her audience. She knew the people from whom she came. She was never guilty of the arrogance that creeps over writers when they become famous," said Keillor, whose more than a dozen books include *Lake Wobegon Days, The Book of Guys, Love Me, Homegrown Democrat* and *Pontoon.*

Drawing laughs, he asked, "What does it take to be a writer of humor? It takes a difficult childhood. If you had a happy childhood, you should go into orthodontics or the priesthood." Later, he advised, "You need to be able to court disaster."

Keillor described Bombeck as a "strong feminist and a devout Catholic" from Dayton, Ohio, who wrote in a universal language. "She didn't write about God. She would write about children. In writing about children, she wrote about God.

"She won the friendship of millions and millions of women and grudgingly of men — even though she said, 'God created man, and I could have done better.'"

Telling illustrative stories and breaking into songs about his hardscrabble childhood in wintry Minnesota, the creator, host and writer of public radio's *A Prairie Home Companion* said that all writing is rooted in compassion — even satire.

Noting that "nothing comes naturally when it involves language," Keillor advised writers to hone their voice.

"You've inherited your voice from other people," he said. "Once you find your voice, stay with it and trust it."

(Spring 2008)

Erma, in Her Own Words

In 1991, I had the opportunity to interview Erma Bombeck for the University of Dayton Quarterly. *At the time, the university's most famous graduate and the country's top female humorist was chronicling life's absurdities three times a week in a syndicated column carried by 700 newspapers, and she had just published her 10th book,* When You Look Like Your Passport Photo, It's Time to Go Home. *I reached Erma at her Arizona home just before she and her family left for a vacation in Costa Rica, and we chatted about traveling, writing, her college days and taking risks. Here are excerpts from our conversation.*

UDQ: Why would anyone who lives in a place called Paradise Valley even want to take a vacation?

Erma (laughing): It's a misnomer, that's why. When the temperature is 122 degrees here, you'll go anywhere.

UDQ: Have you been to Central America before?

Erma: We've never been to Central America. It's just a matter of looking throughout the world and picking spots that aren't hot spots. That's pretty tricky. We subtract the places where we have been — we don't want to go back and see the same place twice because we're getting old — and then eliminate places where it's probably not too safe to travel.

UDQ: You don't keep a journal on these trips. Do you just record your impressions when you get back?

Erma: Exactly. Whatever surfaces when I get home I figure is important enough to remember (laughing).

UDQ: Tell me about your writing process. How do you write? Do you set aside a certain time of the day, and if so, why aren't you writing now?

Erma: I am. You just interrupted me at a page and a half. Discipline is what I do best. I can't imagine any writer saying to you, "I just write when I feel like it." That's a luxury, and that's stupid. The same for writer's block. If you're a professional writer, you write. You don't sit there and wait for sweet inspiration to tap you on the shoulder and say, "now's the time." We meet deadlines. I write for newspapers, and newspapers don't wait for anyone.

You write whether you feel like it, you write whether you've got an idea, you write whether it's Pulitzer Prize material. You just do it; that's it. Discipline is what we're all about. If you don't have discipline, you're not a writer. This is a job for me. I come in every morning at 8 a.m., and I don't leave until 11:30 for lunch. I take a nap, and then I'm back at the typewriter by 1:30, and I write until 5. This happens five, six, seven days a week. I don't see how I can do any less.

UDQ: A deadline is a great motivator, isn't it?

Erma: It is! You can't fool around. A lot of people who want to be writers sit around and say, "You know, when I get the kitchen cleaned up, and when I get the casserole made, when I pick up the kids from school, when I get the carpet cleaned, I'm going to sit down and write." They procrastinate all the time. Writing has to be a priority. I have a son who's a writer in Los Angeles for made-for-television movies. He had a job in an advertising agency, and I told him, "If you're serious, then you have to put it on the line. You have to take a risk. You have to say, 'I am a writer and quit the job.' There comes a time when you have to stop talking and start doing." So he quit the job.

UDQ: Let's talk about your memories of the University of Dayton. You first went to Ohio University before coming here, right?

Erma: It's funny. I got a call the other day from someone in alumni records at OU. I was asked what recollections I had of Ohio University. The recollection I had was that a guidance counselor advised me quite strongly to get out of journalism and become a secretary. It was a kick in the head because I had been working on a newspaper (*The Journal Herald*, Dayton) for a year to earn money for tuition. Then I quit that job to get a college degree. He advised me to get out of journalism, that there was absolutely no hope whatsoever.

UDQ: Because of financial difficulties, you then came home and started to take classes at UD, where you majored in English. You often talk about the value of good teachers. Tell me about someone who had an impact on your life.

Erma: I always come back to one teacher. When you're a writer, one of the things you need is some encouragement. UD was a streetcar college, and I lived at home. I had to have a part-time job in order to go there at all. I wasn't involved in a lot of extra-curricular campus things — pompoms and all that stuff — but I was invited to participate in *The Exponent*, the college magazine. Brother Tom Price ran the thing, and I also had him for a couple of English classes. He said to me, "Why don't you contribute some humor to this?" That was like a breath of fresh air. No one wanted anyone to write humor at that time. It was not exactly something that they lusted for. To make fun of someone or something takes a pretty thick skin.

I started to write humor for *The Exponent*, and one day he said to me three magic words: "You can write." I needed it at that time. It's all I needed as an impetus to keep going, and it sustained me for a very long time. Here's a man who reads *Jane Eyre*, who knows all these things. This man knows what he's talking about. I believed him. You need someone whom you respect to tell you something like that.

UDQ: Particularly when you're young, and you don't have the success that you have now.

Erma: You don't have anything. Writers put it on the line all the time. They have to in order to see how good or how bad they are. It (your writing) goes out there, and they (editors) are going to tell you. They'll let you know in a big hurry if you're good or not. They move right on to the next one. What Brother Tom Price said was important to me.

UDQ: Besides Brother Tom Price, I believe there was a priest here who influenced you to convert to Catholicism.

Erma: Father (Edwin) Leimkuhler, head of the religion department, who just died. I was seeing a lot of faith around me, naturally. You live with it at UD. I was a practicing Protestant, not someone just roaming around. I'm always very insulted when people say to me, "Did you convert for your husband?" That's the stupidest thing I've ever heard in my life. You don't take on something this important for anybody in the world. You don't do that for somebody else; you do it for yourself.

I was curious about the religion. I thought it had such power and strength. So I just wandered into his office one day and told him how I felt. I said, "I'm not committed to this. Don't think for a minute that I'm going to convert. If I ask you a question and you can't plain and simply answer this for me with some kind of rationale, I'm out of here. I'm history." He said, "Fair enough." So I took private instructions with Father Leimkuhler for a lot of months. To me, it was the best way to go. I brought maturity to it; I wasn't just reciting catechism. It was a good time to come to it, and it works for me. It still works for me.

UDQ: When you look back over your life, would you have ever thought this kind of fame awaited you? Did you ever imagine it when you were writing your column for the *Kettering-Oakwood Times* or obituaries for *The Journal Herald* or that column called *The Owl* that you had in high school?

Erma: Even further back than that. Even growing up on Bainbridge Street in the Haymarket District. I took my husband recently to the American Booksellers Association convention. I said, "You've got to see the ABA before I hang it up." We were standing there amidst three floors of nothing but new books. I said, "Now you tell me how am I going to cut through all of this?" The competition is so great. But the book, just two weeks ago, made the bestseller list.

UDQ: Have you had any thoughts of "hanging it up?"

Erma: If I don't have anything more to say, I'll be the first to know that. But I don't see that yet.

(Winter 1991)

2 CULTURES,
2 RELIGIONS,
1 WORLD

Seeing with the Heart

Forget the reporter's notebook. I'd pack a journal if I could go back in time to April 1, 1982. That's the day I first stepped foot in Pakistan — not as a tourist, but as a bride, wondering if this was not some sort of a wild dream.

Imagine getting married just hours after arriving in an exotic land. Repeating your wedding vows in Arabic. Wearing colorful, ceremonial shalwar-kameez. Being suddenly immersed in a large, tight-knit family, one that had already picked out a bride for your husband. And it wasn't you.

We spent five weeks in Pakistan, where Zafar showed me his homeland through his eyes. We strolled through the perfectly manicured Lawrence and Shalimar Gardens, appreciating the British and Persian influences of order and elegance. Visited the Badshahi Mosque, one of the largest and most majestic mosques in the world. Watched the sun set over the Ravi River. Shared a cup of tea with poor yet hospitable villagers in the middle of a dusty road outside Islamabad. Surprised a willing farmer with our plea for a short ride on his camel. Rode gaily painted, three-wheeled rickshaws through chaotic traffic to bazaars and restaurants. Woke each morning either to the wail of a muezzin calling the faithful to prayer or a neighbor's rambunctious rooster announcing the day.

With my reporter's notebook and my husband as a translator, I interviewed teachers, principals and government officials about the state of the developing country's educational system. I wrote a feature story that appeared in *The Guardian* in London as well as the *Christian Science Monitor* and the *Dayton Daily News Magazine.*

It was the first of a series of journalistic pieces, ranging from op-eds to personal essays, from the eyes of an American. After each of our travels to Pakistan, I'd bring home handmade carpets, marble vases, embroidered handiwork — and scribbled pages of observations.

Fresh from journalism school and a stint as a researcher for ABC News in London, I initially viewed Pakistan with the objective eyes of a journalist. But nearly three decades later, my vision has changed.

I've been welcomed into a loving family and given an inside view of everyday moments in a country of surprising paradoxes.

Pakistan still feels like another world, but now it's my world, too.

(Spring 2010)

Somewhere, a Flower Blooms

As the afternoon skies burst open one humid July afternoon, a monsoon rain showers my 7-year-old and his cousins. They romp in the rain as though it were a gigantic backyard sprinkler.

In Pakistan, enthusiasm tends to be dampened by reality: Elsewhere in Lahore, families construct makeshift walls to protect their homes from the almost-daily rains during monsoon season. In a nearby village, hundreds of children die of cholera.

As an American, I'm struck by the dichotomies of everyday life in this developing country. Toyota Land Cruisers share the road with ox-drawn carts loaded with sugar cane and motor scooters carrying entire families.

When Pakistan conducted nuclear tests, people danced jubilantly in the streets. Today, those same streets are often swollen with water because the country has no adequate storm drainage system. And euphoria has been replaced by unease as the economy teeters on collapse.

During our three-week summer visit, Prime Minister Nawaz Sharif froze $11 billion in foreign currency accounts, increased petrol prices 25 percent and urged Pakistanis to sacrifice to help the country live within its means after foreign aid dried up following the nuclear tests. Almost-daily shelling persists in Kashmir, the territory over which Pakistan and India fought two of their three wars in the 50 years since the two countries were sliced out of the subcontinent. The world watches, wondering if these rivals will annihilate each other or broker peace.

Given these many challenges, how can a country built on faith not lose its hope? Perhaps the answer lies, not in the headlines, but in the hearts of Pakistan's people.

In 1947, my husband's family left all of their belongings and gave up an affluent life near New Delhi to start over in a new country created as a homeland for Muslims. This summer, Rizvi family and friends numbering more than 400 gathered at a traditional Islamic prayer service at the family's home in Lahore 40 days after my husband's father died. As we mourned the loss of the 82-year-old patriarch, we celebrated life — and all of its undiscovered possibilities.

A niece is ready to give birth to her first child. A brother wants to enter politics because he thinks he can make a difference in a country that needs honest leadership. A cousin, a self-described "die-hard optimist" and owner of a manufacturing plant, pays 90 rupees out of every 100 he earns in taxes. He could avoid steep taxes as so many others do, but he chooses to pay because "in 10 years, when we get through this, this will be a better country for our children."

And my father-in-law, a retired police officer who adored children — particularly the dozen grandchildren growing up in his house — quietly willed land to a scholarship fund for orphans. For years, with no fanfare or pretension, Aba Jee (a name meaning "dearest father") supported this fund because he knew that education is a way out of poverty.

With grace, he showed us what it means to live your life with meaning.

A poem by Palestinian poet Fadwa Touqan captures Aba Jee and his family's enduring faith and offers a glimpse into the psyche of many Pakistanis:

I ask nothing more
Than to die for my country.
To dissolve and merge with the soil,
To nurture the grass,
To give life to a flower,
That a child of my country will pick.
All I ask
Is to remain in the bosom of my
country.
As soil
Grass
A flower.

To the children's disappointment, the rain abruptly ends just as quickly as it started, and the sun pokes out from behind the clouds. It's cooler and calmer.

Somewhere in Lahore, a family tallies the damage from the storm. Elsewhere, a flower blooms.

(Autumn 1998)

Shock. Grief. Fears. Prayers.

Across the world from each other, in countries torn apart by the terrorist attacks, my niece and I watch the same horrifying images on CNN.

Though from different religious faiths, we speak the same language of grief and fear. We share the bond of a family brought closer together through tragedy.

"We've been watching the coverage, and it still seems like something out of a Hollywood horror flick," she emails from Lahore, the cultural heart of Pakistan near the India border.

"Every day we watch people on TV, holding photos of their loved ones who are missing. It's heartbreaking. No religion in the world preaches killing innocent people in the name of God and taking pride in it."

Yet Pakistanis fear a backlash from religious extremists over their country's decision to help the U.S. in its war against terrorism.

"Pakistan is in a very tough situation. It's a real test of the government and all of us. Generally, people are scared. What if the Third World War begins? We'd be the first ones to perish from the face of the earth," she writes. "On the other hand, even if … Pakistan helps the U.S. get to the Taliban or (Osama) bin Laden, we'll have to go through a chain of religious killings in the country. Taliban-supporting religious groups are already threatening to 'teach a lesson' to the government and retaliating with full force. So, we're in a fix either way."

The planes that ripped through the heart of America have touched our families in ways that most Americans can't fathom.

Our 25-year-old nephew from Pakistan recently arrived in Dayton from Washington, D.C., freshly shaven, wearing Western clothes and shaken by the terrorist attacks. Five passengers made the flight, but his bags were the only ones searched by the FBI as the U.S. tightens security at the nation's airports. That didn't surprise this young lawyer. He knows he looks like he might fit the profile.

Pakistan has moved from obscurity to an international spotlight focused on tracking down bin Laden. Suddenly childhood friends are calling me, worried about our family in Pakistan — a country many Americans would be hard pressed to pinpoint on a map. When we were kids, we couldn't even spell Afghanistan, and now it's part of our daily vocabulary. Our family in Pakistan worries about anti-Muslim sentiment rising up against their son and our children here, while we lose sleep over their safety.

President Gen. Pervez Musharraf has pledged his support, but can the U.S. trust him? He faces the Herculean task of restraining a small but vocal band of militants who back bin Laden while supporting the U.S. in a war on terrorism. It's a defining moment for Musharraf, who seeks legitimacy.

When my family visited Lahore in July, I expected to find people fed up with Musharraf. After all, just days before an ice-breaking summit with neighboring rival India, Musharraf calmly declared himself president and dissolved the Senate, the Parliament and four provincial assemblies.

The move was not met by widespread public outrage. But neither was his bloodless coup nearly two years ago.

That may puzzle those of us who only know democracy. Musharraf is the fourth military ruler to assume the presidency in a country that has been ruled by the military for about half of its history of independence. The last two democratically elected prime ministers have both been accused of corruption, and Pakistanis say they're tired of politicians abusing power. At dinner parties during our two-week visit, we heard doctors, educators and college students praise Musharraf as a "moderate" who has clamped down on corruption and sectarian violence.

He's preached peace, but now some in the country wonder if he has signed his own death warrant by siding with the U.S. over hard-core fundamentalists. Pakistanis, most of whom are moderate Muslims, worry about the fury of extremists who carry signs in English and Urdu and shout slogans of "Long live the Taliban." They worry what a full-scale military attack will mean for their country. They worry about Afghans who are trying to flee their country for safe harbor over the border.

"In the last few days a large number of Afghans have migrated to Pakistan, and their condition is unimaginable," my niece writes. "They were left with nothing more to sell to buy food, and they were dying of starvation. It's the same case back in their country."

In the U.S., children mail donations to President George Bush to help the Afghan children. In Pakistan, children collect food to feed the same children.

And across the world from each other, an American and a Pakistani pray for peace.

(Autumn 2001)

Subject: We're All Safe

With the strength of a tornado, a deadly bomb blast shattered the windows of our family's home in Lahore just a year ago. The terrorist attack had targeted a nearby police building, but shards of glass fell on my frightened niece Sidra in her bed.

"The blast was deafening and terrifying," wrote my niece Fizzah in an email from Pakistan that reached us at dawn before we turned on the morning news. "It was a suicide bombing, with bombers blowing up a van full of explosives."

Her subject line read, "We're All Safe."

Just two months earlier, my nephew Ali Akbar barely escaped being in the vicinity of an attack on the Sri Lankan cricket team bus, which claimed innocent lives and struck a blow against the nation's beloved pastime. International teams no longer travel to Pakistan for matches.

Today, armed militants attacked two mosques in Lahore, killing 80 people, injuring hundreds and taking some hostage in a Taliban-style coordinated attack. Just days earlier, Lahore's High Court suspended access to Facebook because of furor over an internet campaign urging people to post caricatures of Prophet Muhammad.

"We are, I guess, so used to it by now that we have stopped commenting on these issues," Sajjad, another nephew, wrote on my Facebook wall in clear violation of the ban. "I am deeply disappointed with this whole situation, and I just hope that we can see the silver lining soon."

It's hard to believe this is the same city I entered as a nervous bride on April Fools' Day 1982. It seems a lifetime ago that we freely roamed Lahore's chaotic, traffic-choked streets in rickshaws. We soaked in the ambiance of the country's cultural capital, appreciating its carefully tended public gardens, stately colonial-style buildings, colorfully decorated trucks and carefree kite-flying festivals.

Even then, we joked that we feared for our lives. A trip to the bazaar could be harrowing, with Toyotas aggressively jostling for space with horse-drawn tongas and motorized scooters on dusty roads built for another century.

Fast forward to the present: Backed by the U.S. government, Pakistan's military has waged battle with extremists in a campaign that pits the modern world against a militant brand of Islam. It's become too volatile for us to return anytime soon.

I read the headlines, watch televised images of terror — and pray for all the innocent people caught in the crossfire.

These aren't nameless victims. They're my family.

(Spring 2010)

Faces of Pakistan

Pakistan is a country where militants in the idyllic Swat Valley have torched more than 130 girls' schools. Where dozens of suicide bombings — and the assassination of Benazir Bhutto — have rocked civilian life. Where suspected spies are publicly executed and women have very little freedom near the Taliban-infested border with Afghanistan.

It's also a country where my niece and I can don sweatpants and T-shirts and hit the treadmill at the gym. At this upscale coed health club, men wear shorts, treadmills are outfitted with TV screens, and the trainer brings you ice water — a custom so civilized that it should be adopted worldwide.

In my first journey back to my husband's homeland in three summers, I was struck by the contradictory faces of Pakistan. An armed security guard stoically stood watch inside the gate of our family's home in Lahore, a bustling city near the border of India. Under his watchful eye, our boys played a boisterous game of cricket with their cousins in the front yard. In the past two years, he has only shot at a crow, but his somber presence is unsettling.

"Whatever you see is the real Pakistan," says Hasan "Askari" Rizvi, a relative and a political analyst who's writing a book, *Pakistan After 9/11*. "Pakistan used to be a moderate, liberal country. In major urban areas, the situation is more or less like that. Women wear jeans and drive cars. In other parts of the country, you'll see schools for girls being burned. There are still people in this country who don't realize the Taliban are a threat to the existence of this state."

Emboldened, the Taliban are slowly moving from the lawless tribal region, where the militants have found a sanctuary, into the heart of the country.

Just days after we left, a suicide bomber in Lahore killed at least eight during an Independence Day celebration. Twin suicide bombings at a weapons manufacturing plant near the capital of Islamabad took another eight lives.

"They're like a Frankenstein monster," Askari says of the Taliban. "They've changed the direction of their guns from Afghanistan to Pakistan." Yet in numerous conversations with Pakistanis during our 10-day trip to Lahore for our nephew's wedding in August, most didn't talk about the rising tide of violence.

There's little outcry against the Taliban. It's as though atrocities are being committed in some faraway land instead of a mere 300 miles away in a region where armed religious extremists have set up a parallel government and imposed the strictest form of Islamic law.

Some see the war on terror as someone else's war, a war America has waged on Islam. Some believe the Taliban should be placated in case the country needs these warriors for its on-again, off-again conflict with India.

Much as in America, the economy and political future weigh on people's minds. Annual inflation tops an alarming 25 percent. Electricity outages have become so frequent that families buy generators. A fragile democracy appears to be in disarray following the resignation of President Pervez Musharraf, who overthrew the elected government in a bloodless coup in 1999.

Yet it's remarkable how the human spirit triumphs in the face of such uncertainty.

In nightly rehearsal sessions leading up to three days of

elaborate wedding festivities, our nieces and nephews gathered around their cousin, Sarah, as she played the *dholki*, a traditional barrel-shaped drum, and led them in joyous wedding songs. They dressed our sons in long, embroidered coats called *sherwanis* and Aladdin-style *khussas* shoes. As part of one offbeat ritual, the cousins stole the groom's shoes and demanded he pay them or go barefoot.

This face of Pakistan — ordinary people finding joy in everyday moments — remains invisible to most of the world in the face of the militant extremism that now dominates the headlines.

As we bade emotional farewells to our family, our younger son, Ali, impulsively gave an enormous bear hug to Tassaduq, the security guard quietly standing in the distance. We erupted in laughter. Caught off guard, Tassaduq broke into a wide smile.

That's one face of Pakistan I'll never forget.

(Autumn 2008)

A New World

It seemed our world collapsed overnight.

One moment, we're gulping down dinner, scurrying to yet another soccer game, trying to steal time for ourselves. The next moment, we're watching in horror as our 5-year-old takes two small plastic toy planes and crashes them into pretend towers.

"New York is falling apart," he says with simple child logic.

Suddenly, stealing time isn't good enough anymore. We long to go back in time, take a tumble to those untroubled days of our courtship in London when we strolled through Kensington Gardens on idle Sundays that stretched before us with the promise and beauty of the carefully tended perennials. The world we dreamed for our children offered the same predictable beauty and manicured order.

Our family would settle for reliving last summer when we maneuvered up a steep, winding road into the Himalaya Mountains in Pakistan and discovered a stunningly beautiful world that rivals Switzerland's breathtaking ranges. Here, in this hot, dusty, impoverished country, I've discovered an unexpected beauty and a rich family life I couldn't have predicted nearly 20 years ago when we repeated marriage vows in Arabic and topped that off with a second wedding in a Catholic church — "just to make sure it took," we'd joke to friends.

Today, Pakistan contends with war on the Afghanistan border, a near-war on the Indian border and a cultural war — one that has pitted the culture of the West against Islam. Villagers may still gently prod goats up that mountain pass outside Islamabad, but this is not the same pastoral portrait. The State Department warned U.S. citizens about traveling to the region after a *Wall Street Journal* reporter was kidnapped by a splinter fanatic group. Though the government is a staunch American ally, some people believe extremists are harboring terrorist Osama bin Laden.

"It's a whole new world," my 17-year-old nephew Ather says in an email. "The time we spent together in July seems to be in another era."

How can a few months constitute another era? How can "one man ruin it for everyone?" asks my husband, Zafar, an American citizen who has avoided air travel since Sept. 11 because he doesn't want to be looked at with suspicion simply because he's a Muslim. For a man who moved to the U.S. with hesitation because it was unfamiliar and it meant leaving family behind, he now bristles when anyone suggests he's not as American as the township trustee who lives across the street.

For months, we've plowed on, heads down, burying ourselves in work and the kids, deadlines and commitments. Keeping busy was the perfect antidote for pain and a way to avoid talking about what really matters.

But one January weekend we bolt out of work early, leaving the kids with kindhearted friends who know we need time alone. We drive to a bed-and-breakfast tucked in the tiny town of Aurora, Indiana, on the Ohio River, where, like everywhere else in this vast country, American flags drape the landscape.

We discovered this quaint, restored 1860s Gothic Revival house last winter during a getaway journey. Nestled in rolling hills within walking distance of the river and a historic white-washed church with a graceful spire, it's a sliver of Americana, an idyllic place that beckons you to capture time, hold it — and treasure it.

People here don't like to lock their doors. Neighbors banter with one another. It's a throwback to another era.

On a lazy Saturday morning, the innkeepers serve up an ample helping of conversation with Italian omelets, homemade scones and strong coffee. They're curious, being archaeologists by training. Maybe living in a small town gives you more time to ponder the world at large, creating an intimacy with strangers who sleep in your beds and drink your coffee. On our earlier visit, we analyzed America's 2000 national election fiasco. Now the conversation turns to more troubling times. It's hard to believe we once cared so passionately about hanging chads.

The morning's headline sparks talk of bin Laden's whereabouts. Is he dead or alive? Is peace in the world possible when one man and his cult of followers can turn it upside down overnight?

After breakfast, as a soft morning snowfall transforms the town into a winter postcard, we walk along the river in peaceful silence and draw in the cold air. One weekend away won't heal our hurting world, but time away together has helped. As we head home, we are ready to keep putting our world back together, relying on two decades of counting on one another — and offering that same loving resolve to our children.

(Winter 2002)

'His Ghost Haunts Both Sides'

Within hours after arriving in Lahore, Pakistan, this summer, three people asked me if I was scared.

Like many Americans, I don't feel as safe in my own country anymore — let alone another nation where Westerners have been targeted. As tensions simmered after 9/11, *Wall Street Journal* reporter Danny Pearl was kidnapped and murdered in Karachi, and two Americans were killed and several more injured in a bombing at an Islamabad church. This sun-drenched country along the Arabian Sea has never been a hot tourist spot, but the State Department is urging Westerners to keep a low profile.

It's not just Americans who are edgy. Pakistanis are shaken by extremists in their own ranks. When Pakistan's military ruler Gen. Pervez Musharraf courageously opted to side with the United States in its fight against terrorism, the government found itself rooting out hundreds of Taliban and al-Qaida supporters and contending with anti-American demonstrations. Pakistanis widely believe that Osama bin Laden is probably hiding somewhere along the lawless, remote tribal area between Pakistan and Afghanistan.

"We don't know if Osama bin Laden is dead or alive, but his ghost haunts both sides," says Hasan "Askari" Rizvi, a relative and political analyst often sought by the international media. "For the U.S., he's a symbol of evil. For those who support him, he's seen as a hero. The extremists are small in number, but they're loud and organized. With five people shooting their guns, you can create hell in the streets.

"There's the fear of the unknown. You never know when a

bomb will explode."

What brought us to this land of uncertainty? For more than two decades, we've made the journey to my husband's homeland because of a rich family life that has nurtured us the way the July monsoon rains enliven the parched land.

This country cherishes its children and reveres its elderly. We look forward to eating sweet mangoes and hearing the familiar ribbing between brothers who exaggerate stories from their childhood. Although I'm not Muslim, I appreciate hearing the rhythmic call for prayer five times a day. It's a constant reminder that so much of what we worry about is not in our hands.

Still, it's hard not to worry. Symbols of unease abound. The stately British Library is closed, armed guards at its gate. Not far away, a guard with a rifle pointed at visitors sits perched on a truck on the road leading to the American Embassy.

We spot an armed motorcyclist clad in a black T-shirt emblazoned with the phrase, "No Fear." He works for a private security company that hires guards for school functions and events. Security guards are not a new sight in Lahore, but there are more of them. While we've grown accustomed to being greeted by a guard toting a rifle at an upscale restaurant or outside the gate of a cousin's bungalow, it's now common to be startled by security personnel at the gas pump and spot armed men at mosques and churches.

Before 9/11, few Americans could find Pakistan on a map, though the two countries have shared an on-again, off-again relationship for decades.

Pakistanis will readily tell you they believe the United States abandoned them after the Soviets were driven out of Afghanistan in 1989.

They're still bitter about sanctions imposed on Pakistan in the 1990s when it became a nuclear power, and they're annoyed the United States has not stepped in to help solve its dispute with

India over who controls Kashmir.

But the United States has written off more than $1 billion of debt, rescheduled loan payments and offered a $3 billion aid package for the country's role in the war on terrorism.

Foreign reserves have risen to a record $11 billion. The charismatic Musharraf, who took power in a bloodless coup in 1999, remains popular at home and with the United States — despite anti-American sentiment in the country.

"The people at the top are moderates. They're not isolated from the international community," said Mohsin Rizvi, a cousin who owns an electronics factory.

"Musharraf takes a moderate approach to life and religion. We are fed up with the extremism, what I call the CNN and BBC Syndrome. There's more value in footage of violent demonstrations, even though it represents a small portion of the population."

Still, the American-educated engineer notes that support for the United States breaks down according to education level. "If you interview people whose education level is below 10 years, they're pro-Osama. If you talk to educated people, no one favors Osama."

Pakistan's illiteracy rate hovers above 50 percent. I remember the young servant girl who brought us drinks when we visited someone's home, the children weaving carpets in a factory, the young boy begging outside the bakery. What chance do they have of receiving the same education as my sons and their cousins — and viewing the world through that lens?

As we board the plane to fly home, their faces haunt me.

(Autumn 2003)

An Idealistic Tax Collector

It's no wonder that a record-low number of Pakistanis turned out for the February 1997 parliamentary elections: Having nine prime ministers in 10 years has taken its toll on even the most optimistic of Pakistan's 130 million citizens.

Nawaz Sharif, dismissed as prime minister in 1993 on charges of corruption, in February succeeded Benazir Bhutto, who was ousted twice on the same allegations. It's a development that would startle those comfortable with Western-style democracy, but it doesn't turn heads in Pakistan.

"This is Pakistani politics. Anything can happen," said a college student with a shrug.

It's true. During our periodic visits to the Asian subcontinent to visit my husband's family, we've witnessed military rule, the overnight collapse of a democratic government and continual charges of mismanagement. People have come to expect political instability, corruption and broken campaign promises.

That's why Zia Haider Rizvi's almost-childlike enthusiasm, his belief that he can change the system, is so refreshing.

"I used to pray to Allah, if I had a chance, I could make a difference. Like a fairy tale, I got my chance," says Rizvi, a successful tax attorney tapped to serve briefly as special assistant to the chief minister of Punjab in Pakistan's caretaker government after Bhutto was dismissed for the second time.

About 60 percent of the nation's populace lives in Punjab, Pakistan's largest province. My husband's cousin headed the excise and taxation department, an agency with a reputation he describes as one of the most corrupt in the country.

"I called the tax inspectors a cheat to their faces," he said, recalling his first meeting with the staff. "The tax collectors are richer than all of us. They were sharing the loot. What I've tried to do is eliminate the bottlenecks and create accountability for the assessors. If you're a tax assessor, you cannot drive up in the most expensive car when everyone knows your salary is only $150 (a month)."

Rizvi urged the government to adopt a single tax policy to give companies protection against double taxation, auction off special automobile license plate numbers to generate additional revenue and grant more than 6,000 widows a speedy property-tax exemption — a right ensnared in bureaucratic paperwork.

Rizvi also promised the tax collectors that he would work to increase their monthly wages and promised them a 1 percent bonus if they met tax-collection goals and treated people fairly. Within a month, the province collected 1.75 billion rupees over what is normally collected, he noted with pride.

Yet Rizvi believes Pakistanis will continue to dodge taxes.

"There's no trust among the government and the public at large," he said. "We haven't had a politically stable government, and the ones we've had have thought about benefiting themselves instead of the country. People think, 'Why should we pay taxes if it's going into someone else's pocket?' That has to change."

Pakistan, carved out of India as a separate homeland for Muslims in 1947, stands at a pivotal point in its history. According to the Associated Press, defense spending accounts for a third of the country's $13 billion budget, and debt servicing eats up another third. The International Monetary Fund has provided emergency and long-term loans but has withheld payments in the past year because the country has teetered on bankruptcy. Sectarian violence in major cities such as Karachi and Lahore has threatened law and order, and many agree that corruption is a deep-rooted problem.

Still, Rizvi, whose late father served as a minister after the partition from India, is convinced that Pakistan has the potential to evolve into what pundits call an Asian tiger. He pointed to his own success in three months, heralded in dozens of newspaper clippings, as proof that change can happen: "This can be done in Pakistan at every level, provided the person in authority has ability and enjoys a reputation of being above-board."

His response to people who ask why they should pay taxes when the government can't always provide basic services such as good roads?

"I tell them, 'It's your country. You are living in a free land, breathing your own air. Even if your road is broken, contribute something to your country.'"

(Winter 1997)

Season of Discontent

If the recent mysterious airplane crash that killed Pakistani dictator Mohammed Zia ul-Haq is confirmed as sabotage, it wouldn't be terribly surprising.

This whodunit rivals the best of American television's night-time cliffhangers. A cast of suspects, ranging from political opponents within the country to members of Zia's military regime to people with "foreign involvement," are all center stage as investigators try to unravel why Zia's C-130 military plane crashed in a remote area of Pakistan.

For Zia's opponents in this overwhelmingly Muslim nation, it's been more than a decade of discontent — and some fear. With the strength of the armed forces behind him, Zia came to power in a 1977 military coup that toppled Zulfikar Ali Bhutto, the only democratically elected leader the country had known in its 41-year existence.

Later, Zia hanged Bhutto on what Bhutto's daughter, Benazir, called a fabricated charge against her father of conspiracy to murder a political opponent.

The United States has been a willing ally of Zia, at times casting a blind eye to human rights violations, such as public floggings. Zia had shown strong support for Afghan rebels battling the Soviet Union, and Pakistan has strategic importance in global politics.

I became a Pakistan watcher in 1980 when I met my future husband in London. Since then, we've traveled back to his home-land twice. Days before our flight touched down in Karachi this summer, Zia had dissolved the national and provincial assemblies and ousted his hand-picked prime minister. He promised new elections in 90 days, a restoration of law and order, and a quicker implementation of Islamic reforms.

Braced for public outrage or at least unrest, we were surprised to experience a wait-and-see calm that, despite a record-breaking heat spell, seemed to pervade the country. Zia's ban of all public demonstrations might have been the reason, but often-violent street demonstrations and other signs of civil unrest have marred the military general's 11-year rule.

Privately, some of Zia's opponents expressed confidence that the dictator's rule was nearing a close. A doctor in the capital city of Islamabad told me that the dissolution of Zia's civilian government, the only step he had made toward much-promised democracy, spelled the beginning of the end for the military government. If the ruler kept his promise to hold an election, the country would vote him out of office. Zia's sole key to remaining in control lay in continued U.S. support — what many Pakistanis believe to be the general's only staying power.

On the other side of the debate, a perplexed Zia adversary and successful lawyer saw no end in sight to the Zia dynasty. Noting a terrorist group's unsuccessful 1982 attempt to shoot down Zia's plane with a surface-to-air missile, he said, "By the grace of God, the man has always survived."

In the end, however, foul play appears to have decided Zia's fate. While thousands mourned his death, it was a subdued crowd, a muted grief. As expected, the Pakistan People's Party, Zia's staunchest opposition, led by Benazir Bhutto, showed no restraint in its reaction to the president's sudden death.

"Internationally, Zia may be remembered as the man who stood up to the Soviets after they entered Afghanistan," the PPP said in a statement. "But in Pakistan, he will be remembered as the man who illegally seized power, and after 11-and-a-half years of repressive rule, left behind nothing but death and mortgages, hunger and unemployment, exploitation and discrimination, drugs and corruption."

Zia's death gives the country a welcomed chance to pursue democratic rule again. In a heartening move, government officials followed Pakistan's constitution and swore in Senate Chairman Ghulam Ishaq Khan as acting president.

Khan promises that elections will proceed as scheduled, but there appears to be no real heir apparent to Zia's throne. Zia's fired prime minister, Mohammed Khan Junejo, is expected to rally the Muslim League Party in a fight for the presidency. The American- and British-educated Bhutto, who spent five years under house arrest during the Zia regime, has been likened to the Philippines' Corazon Aquino — someone who has the ability to relentlessly hound a dictator out of office. While Bhutto draws enthusiastic crowds wherever she speaks and appears to have genuine popular support, her platform is based on politics heavy with revenge and light on substance. With Zia gone, there's some question whether she's lost her reason to fight.

The world of Pakistani politics is volatile and often dangerous, evidenced by three successful coups in four decades. If history doesn't repeat itself as it has done so often in Pakistan's short life span, the country's "baby boomers" (those born after the partition from India) may get their chance to decide the future of their country, either at the ballot box or on the campaign trail.

It's a pivotal moment.

(Summer 1988)

Learning to Walk

As Wajiha Anwar dickered the price of an antique with a shop-keeper in one of Lahore's bustling bazaars, Pakistan endured another one of its all-too-familiar military coups.

"We were bargaining the price, and he said, 'Why don't you pay me more? The government has just been overthrown and martial law has been imposed.' He was so jubilant. I was shocked to see his reaction," said the young lawyer.

Just days before an ice-breaking summit with neighboring rival India, Pakistan's military ruler Gen. Pervez Musharraf declared himself president and dissolved the Senate, the Parliament and four provincial assemblies.

Although the move provoked blanket condemnation by the international community, it was not met with widespread public outrage in Pakistan. Why? The last two democratically elected prime ministers were both accused of corruption, and Pakistanis say they're tired of politicians abusing power.

"I don't like (military generals), but for some reason I like Musharraf. When he talks, he talks from the heart," said Mahboob Jaffery, a doctor in the capital city of Islamabad.

"We've had (democratically elected) Benazir Bhutto twice, Nawaz Sharif twice. This can't be any worse," said Muhammad Razi Mirza, principal of Ziaret College of Technology.

Musharraf is the fourth military ruler to assume the presidency in a country that has been ruled by the military for about half of its history of independence. He heads a Muslim nation of 140 million people that stretches from the Arabian Sea to some of the world's most striking mountain ranges.

"People don't dislike Musharraf," agreed Hasan "Askari" Rizvi, a political analyst often sought out by international media for his views on Pakistan's musical-chairs style of politics. "People have been alienated by the way the political leaders handled affairs when they were in power. ... But people still want a democratic system. There's a very strong desire for that. They generally won't favor a long military rule in Pakistan."

Musharraf has promised national elections in October 2002, yet banned all political activity, such as public meetings and rallies. That hasn't stopped veteran democracy champion Nawabzada Nasrullah Khan from speaking his mind, from risking arrest.

"I've never been in power. I've only been in prison," said Khan, pausing to smoke a hookah pipe in a sparsely furnished office that doubles as his bedroom.

Khan has spent decades trying to bring a stable brand of democracy to the country. Now in his 80s, he has formed the Alliance for the Restoration of Democracy, an umbrella of the country's 16 major political parties. During the biggest crackdown on political activity since the military took power, troops arrested 1,600 activists, including 298 political leaders. They placed Khan under house arrest. During the last military regime, he said he spent five years, on and off, in jail.

In a country where security guards frame the doorways of posh restaurants, office buildings and bungalows, no watchman protects the elder statesman. He preaches nonviolence and enjoys such widespread respect that Musharraf sought him out before traveling to a summit between Pakistan and neighboring India. He wanted to hear Khan's views on a wide range of issues, including the dispute over which country controls Kashmir, the beautiful Himalayan region where violence between the two nations has erupted over five decades.

Despite that gesture, Khan is wary of the dictator. "This is not the age for military rule. It sticks out like a sore thumb in the world today," he said. "It's not good for the future of the country. ... How can democracy emerge from the barrel of a gun? It has to come from consensus."

Rizvi, who just returned to Pakistan after four years as a visiting professor at Columbia University, is more pragmatic. "Democracy may not work here in the way it works in the developed countries," he said, though without giving up hope that popular rule might eventually work. "In a democracy, at least people start shouting after a time."

Khan, the country's staunchest supporter of democracy, doesn't raise his voice, but his message is clear. "Whenever a dictator imposes martial law, it's validated by the judiciary. When he goes, we decide he's a usurper. ... This has been our constant behavior," he said.

Wearing traditional Pakistani dress of shalwar-kameez and sporting a day-old beard, Khan talked quietly about his life's work to plant democratic ideals in a country rooted in political upheaval. Given his age, his health (he wears a pacemaker) and the odds against success, why does he keep at it?

"If you don't let your baby walk for 10 or 15 years, he'll never walk. If you let him try to walk, he may stumble, he may get injured in the process, but he will eventually start walking," he said.

(Summer 2001)

FAITH

Why What You Dream Matters

A familiar voice broke the spell. "Are we having any luck with this?"

The answer was plain on the face of film director Ron Hamad, clearly moved as he wrapped up a 90-minute remote recording session with Ramón Estévez.

Better known by his film name Martin Sheen, Estévez loaned his voice — what Hamad described as "a deep, quiet inner voice" — to a five-minute film about the University of Dayton.

Estévez, a Dayton native who never lost touch with his Ohio hometown after he became a celebrity, didn't rush into the Indigo Ranch studio in Malibu and race through the script, even though he started the session by asking, "Want to record one in case we get lucky?"

Instead, he patiently offered dozens of versions in an effort to capture the cadence of a piece designed to inspire alumni and friends to support the school's aspirations for the 21st century.

"I want to feel like you're talking to me and I'm spellbound by you," Hamad told the actor. As Estévez slowly delivered the words, the script's poetry leapt to life:

This is how we connect to each other,
what we give to the world.
Ourselves
Honed to a fine commitment of the spirit.
This is why our dreams of the future are actual,
Why what you dream matters.
We've always known this.

Change that makes a real future
rises from the value of being connected …
This is who we are,
Members of one family called to act in service
To each human life
And so,
In service to the world.

Enveloped by the richness of his voice, we grew quiet, caught in the spell of a masterful delivery. Two thousand miles away, he mistook the silence for discomfort. At one point, he said apologetically, "I do tend to get complacent and fall in love with my voice. The problem with me is that I get locked into something and fall in love with it and can't let go."

Not a startling confession from a man who is passionate about the causes he believes in. He calls himself a Christian activist and has never been afraid to sleep in the cold to demonstrate solidarity with the homeless or get himself arrested for blocking the entrance of a company that conducts nuclear weapons research. He agreed to provide the film's voiceover in exchange for a small donation to the San Carlos Foundation, which he helped start in 1983 to provide health and educational assistance to refugees and others living in extreme poverty in the developing world, particularly Central America.

One of 10 children from a Catholic immigrant family, he grew up on Brown Street in the shadow of the University of Dayton, where his father wanted him to continue his education after graduation from nearby Chaminade High School, now Chaminade Julienne. Both schools were founded by the Marianist religious order to educate for service, justice and peace.

Still, that wasn't enough to persuade him. As he told us at the end of the taping, he had perhaps "the lowest score on record" for his college entrance exams — and besides, he added, "I wanted to go to New York."

And so he did. He moved to the big city and began building an acting career, but he also discovered the work of Catholic activist Dorothy Day. Inspired by her and by his faith, Estévez became committed to social justice. These two strands of his life have repeatedly come together, now in a small favor for his hometown university.

He never attended the school, but he shares its dream of service — and that is what matters.

(Winter 1997)

Postscript: In 2015, Ramón Estévez fulfilled his father's dream when he received an honorary Doctor of Humane Letters degree from the University of Dayton during the spring commencement ceremony. "It's like being canonized," he said, to laughter.

Speak Softly and Be Heard

One, Jewish. One, Christian.

One survived the Holocaust. The other led a university. Both impart life lessons on leadership and faith.

Elie Wiesel, winner of the Nobel Peace Prize, and Brother Raymond L. Fitz, the longest-serving president in University of Dayton history, inspire us by their quiet example. Both have made a permanent mark in the world and can sit back. Yet they continue to stand up against injustice.

Wiesel teaches at Boston University and speaks on campuses around the country. One of a dwindling number of concentration camp survivors, he has no plans to slow down.

"How can one stop? We live in such strange times. I feel obligated. ... There are so many injustices in the world. It would be immoral not to take a stand," he told University of Dayton students when he spoke as part of the 2009-10 Diversity Lecture Series.

Addressing a wide range of issues from genocide to suicide bombers to a two-state solution in the Middle East, Wiesel offered pointed observations on the growing discord in the public square and the rise of extremism around the globe.

"There's a resurgence among the extreme, extreme right that I find offensive and could lead to violence. Some people are even calling our president Hitler," he said quietly, disbelief in his voice. "I don't like this atmosphere. We must learn something from the Holocaust. No more racism. No more hatred. No more injustice. ... With every fiber in my being,

I'm against fanaticism. A fanatic is against dialogue because he only hears himself."

Wiesel speaks very softly, but his words speak volumes.

"I don't like yelling. I believe in whispers. To quote King Solomon, 'Speak softly; you will be heard.'"

Fitz, the University's first Ferree Professor of Social Justice, would be the first to describe himself as an introvert. Since stepping down as president in 2002, he's shied away from the microphone, preferring to teach and work quietly behind the scenes.

So, when he stood up to address an overflow crowd in the Immaculate Conception Chapel at a Mass celebrating the Golden Jubilee of his first vows as a Marianist, you could feel the anticipation.

With equal parts humility and sincerity — dashed with a sprinkling of humor — Fitz singled out the influences of family, faculty and friends, saving his most heartfelt remarks for the poorest children in Dayton. He's worked tirelessly to support urban education and child protection reform in Dayton over decades.

"I have seen firsthand the hopelessness and desperation of children and families who experience extreme poverty," he said, his voice breaking. "These experiences have been a gift — a painful gift — but a gift that has allowed me to see the face of God in a new way."

Listening to words spoken from the heart, I remembered the way Brother Ray described the statues of Mary on campus as symbolic of his Marianist vocation. In the mother of Jesus, he once told me, he sees "a faith that is generous and willing to risk anew, a faith that journeys with others and offers a warm welcome, a faith that is in solidarity with the poor and the powerless."

By their lives, Wiesel and Fitz teach us you don't have to raise your voice to be heard. But you must speak up.

In Wiesel's immortal words, "To remain silent and indifferent is the greatest sin of all."

(Summer 2010)

Roman Holiday

Maybe this is what Mecca feels like, I thought as I jostled for space in St. Peter's Square with tens of thousands of the faithful.

Muslims try to visit Saudi Arabia's Mecca, the holiest city in Islam, at least once during their lives. All roads may lead to Rome, as the old saying goes, but unless it's part of a tour through Italy, most Catholics don't make any special effort to visit the spiritual center of their religion.

Yet 125 Daytonians found a reason to embark on a pilgrimage to Rome, drawn to the holy city by Pope John Paul II's beatification of Father William Joseph Chaminade. The courageous French priest escaped arrest, imprisonment and possible death at the guillotine during the French Revolution to found lay Catholic communities and a new religious order. He is now just one step away from sainthood.

In Dayton, Chaminade's influence is felt in classrooms at the University of Dayton, the halls of Chaminade Julienne High School and the pews of Emmanuel Church, where the Marianist religious order quietly and humbly carries out his 18th-century mission.

Many in our tour group — which included an eclectic mix of priests and brothers, professors and administrators, even a non-Catholic Black family and a curious agnostic law professor — expressed surprise at the unexpected swell of emotion we felt surrounded by 100,000 people outside St. Peter's Basilica.

We arrived 90 minutes early for the beatification ceremony and Mass only to find ourselves in a standing-room-only section of sun-soaked St. Peter's Square. We staked out a front-row spot behind the sea of seats and politely held our ground despite the efforts of several enthusiastic Italian latecomers to secure a better view.

I described the scene as a Roman Woodstock. English professor Brian Conniff labeled it a mosh pit, while physics professor Mike O'Hare said the charged atmosphere felt like an NCAA Final Four game.

Perhaps Joan Wagner, director of Marianist activities at the University of Dayton, offered the most charitable observation of the chaotic scene: "You had the press of the crowd — everyone wanted their place in the midst of this holy celebration — contrasted with the sanctity and holiness of the experience." Once the ceremony started, the mood switched from boisterous to solemn.

I couldn't help but notice these kinds of contrasts in Rome, which one tour guide described as a city of optical illusions. After strolling through the bronze Holy Door at majestic St. Peter's Basilica — a portal opened only during Jubilee years every quarter-century — we spotted a monk, head bowed in silent prayer, as a family posed for a photo in front of one of the 120 altars. A religious procession marched past the *Pietà*, Michelangelo's famous sculpture of Mary holding a lifeless Jesus, parting groups of tourists like a modern-day Moses at the Red Sea. Outside, a street vendor peddled, "Rosaries for a dollar!"

Yet in the midst of what one priest described as a circus atmosphere, we began to shed our tourist demeanors and become pilgrims on a journey of faith. Tears streaked down the cheeks of Monalisa Mullins, a faculty member in the UD philosophy department who converted to Catholicism at Easter, as she watched rays of light from the basilica's dome cast a soft glow on an altar. "I'm absolutely overwhelmed," she said. "It's magnificent beyond belief."

Others felt similar astonishment when Pope John Paul II traveled within inches of the Dayton group in his open-air popemobile following the ceremony. Still others, waving their Chaminade scarves in unison and offering Latin responses they last uttered at Mass as children, felt the surge of camaraderie you might enjoy with strangers during the seventh game of the World Series — only this time the faces surrounding them came from countries all over the world.

Those are the images that will remain etched on our hearts. In a city steeped in religious tradition, many of us discovered our roots. We had become pilgrims.

(Autumn 2000)

Faith in Humanity

"There was a suicide bombing today," my brother-in-law matter-of-factly announced after the failed assassination attempt on the life of Pakistan's prime minister-designate.

He expressed neither surprise nor outrage. While Americans are still reeling from the shock of 9/11, Pakistanis have resigned themselves to terrorist attacks and warnings from militant extremists who have hijacked more than the people's religion; they're trying to rob people of their faith in the future.

In Lahore, the sun-soaked cultural center of Pakistan that's home to 7 million people, there are no color-coded warnings, no efforts to avoid the bazaar or mosque. People continue to ride buses and enjoy high tea at a popular gathering spot. People live in the moment. You walk past armed guards into restaurants teeming with people. Street chefs cook spicy chicken dishes at crowded outdoor cafes long after midnight. Kites, though officially illegal here because of electrocution risks, dot the late-afternoon skies in a show of defiance and a symbol of carefree living.

Stopping by the Pearl Continental Hotel for dinner, we were detained by a dozen guards with rifles who popped open the hood of the car and searched the trunk before allowing us to park and walk through a metal detector. When we learned the lame-duck prime minister was due there for a wedding, one person in our party said, "Don't worry. They won't waste a bullet on him."

The U.S. State Department has asked Americans to defer travel here because of a spate of terrorist attacks. We're advised to keep a low profile, avoid crowds, stay with local families — hide out, in other words.

The military government has rooted out and arrested more than 500 Taliban and al-Qaida supporters and sympathizers. Terrorist plots detailed on a computer seized in a recent raid in Pakistan prompted U.S. officials to beef up security at financial institutions in New York, Washington, D.C., and northern New Jersey.

Just hours after the announcement of the arrest of an al-Qaida suspect sought in connection with the 1998 bombing attacks on U.S. embassies in Tanzania and Kenya, a young man ran through a ring of security guards into the armored Mercedes of Shaukat Aziz, the prime minister-in-waiting. This was the failed assassination attempt my brother-in-law so blithely referred to.

"Your apprehension about coming here can't be ruled out completely," my husband's oldest brother told me when I expressed doubts about this summer's annual trip to visit family. "Even we ourselves feel unsafe in this country."

But in Pakistan, people carry on in the face of uncertainty. To most, the reverent strains of the call to prayer five times daily inspire the faithful to put their trust in a power greater than themselves. Yet for others, it invokes a call to arms.

Pakistanis blame Americans for arming right-wing Islamist groups during the Cold War when the Soviets were driven out of Afghanistan. Many of these groups formed al-Qaida.

Military generals have ruled Pakistan for most of its existence, but even the army is having trouble overpowering fundamentalists in an impoverished land where more than half the citizens are illiterate.

"Gen. Pervez Musharraf's policies have strengthened the same religious groups that he's fighting against. That's a contradiction," observes Hasan "Askari" Rizvi, a relative and a political analyst often sought out by the international media.

"He will not be able to change the environment without allowing liberal values. Education is important, but so is the content. Teachers in government schools talk about creating the ideal Islamic society. There is no ideal Islamic society. They should be teaching about human rights, liberal values and tolerance."

How can a country with faith as its foundation not lose its hope?

I don't have to look very far to see what Pakistan's future could be.

One of my husband's brothers is fighting to restore democracy in his homeland. Another is writing the country's first handbook on anticorruption legal procedures. A niece teaches literature — from Shakespeare to Toni Morrison — at a private high school because she believes "teachers affect eternity."

Over cups of tea in the homes of educated professionals across Lahore, Pakistanis are quick to assure the nervous that suicide bombers are not true Muslims.

"This is not our culture," sighed my husband's childhood friend who is now the law secretary for the state of Punjab. "These people are the desperate class."

Just as the summer monsoon rains offer respite from the stifling heat and a neighbor's peacock startles me with the sheer beauty of its brilliant blue and green feathers, I want to embrace the possible.

I want to believe that in the dangerous game playing out on the world stage in Pakistan, humanity will prevail.

(Summer 2004)

The Ant and the Apple

During a socially distanced parking lot lunch, my friend Emily told me about the fear her young son had conveyed at 3 o'clock that morning.

"How does an ant eat an apple?" Jackson asked.

"One bite at a time, buddy," she responded.

We laughed, not saying out loud what we were both likely thinking: that with faith, even the insurmountable can be conquered.

A year into living with the coronavirus, faith is helping me find grace in the small moments that gobsmack you — a child's innocent question, the way sunlight dapples through the trees, the random kindness of grocery store clerks, a Zoom gathering with old friends.

"Grace is what changes us, heals us and heals our world," wrote author Anne Lamott. "To summon grace, say, 'Help,' and then buckle up."

Amen.

One day I'm wrapping up final details for a workshop that will bring hundreds of writers from around the country to the University of Dayton, and the next day I've shelved it. Swallowing fear, I eventually take a leap of faith and transform the event into a virtual gathering.

Weeks later, as the pandemic surges, my husband passes a battery of heart tests only to hear the startling news he has COVID-19. Tapping into a reservoir of faith, I silently pray for his recovery. One by one, other friends hear the same diagnosis. Most of these cases are mild, but five of my husband's relatives and an elderly neighbor die.

While I haven't ventured back to Sunday Mass since the lockdown began, I'm finding solace in solitude, prayer and reflection — and I'm not the only one. According to a Pew Research Center study, Americans were three times more likely to report that their religious faith had grown stronger during the pandemic.

I've embarked on my own spiritual pilgrimage through long daily walks that fill my soul. In the crunch of leaves on a trail, in the sight of waves on a lake, in the singsong of birds, I feel God's presence in a new way. Gratitude fills my heart. My loved ones have survived an emotional roller coaster of a year when over half a million Americans and counting have died of this capricious virus and innumerable others have lost jobs.

Life doesn't come with an extended warranty that protects us from what's awaiting around the bend, but faith gives us the courage to embrace life's mysteries with hope. As I drive to the Dayton Convention Center for my first vaccine, I hear The Byrds sing "Turn Turn Turn" on the radio. It's another moment of grace, and I quietly sing along:

> *To everything turn, turn, turn*
> *There is a season turn, turn, turn*
> *And a time to every purpose under heaven*

I feel an unexpected rush of emotion as dozens of us stream into a ballroom that's been turned into a makeshift vaccination clinic. With row after row of chairs spaced safely six feet apart, I'm #1,305 out of 2,000 of my Dayton neighbors receiving a dose of hope that March day.

It's the parable of the ant and the apple playing out before my eyes in real time. With one shot at a time, and a measure of faith, we'll conquer this virus.

(Spring 2021)

Words of Thanks

Writing is an act of courage. I'm forever indebted to my family, friends and colleagues who gently, yet persistently, encouraged me to face the blank page and tease words from my heart. You are my muses.

I owe a special debt of gratitude to Julie Fanselow for her editing chops. With careful attention to details and flow, she made the pieces stronger. Julie Lonneman's gorgeous, graceful illustrations capture the spirit behind the stories. My eagle-eye proofreaders — Mary McCarty, Maureen Schlangen and Deborah McCarty Smith — are more than beautiful writers themselves; they are dear friends.

When I reached out to David Braughler at Braughler Books with publishing questions, he readily took on this project and guided its production every step of the way. Together, we are donating proceeds from book sales to the Erma Bombeck Writers' Workshop endowment fund, which keeps the workshop affordable for writers. Thank you, David, for believing in this book — and for bringing it into the world.

Book designer Craig Ramsdell created a simple, elegant look that ties the book together in an engaging way. My heartfelt appreciation to Frank Pauer, Gina Gray and Dani Johnson, who took the time to offer invaluable feedback on the cover design.

A number of these pieces appeared in some form in the *University of Dayton Magazine* or its predecessor, *University of Dayton Quarterly*. Thanks to Tom Columbus, Michelle Tedford, Matt Dewald and Deborah McCarty Smith — all extraordinary editors — for cutting me down to size over the years. I value your editing expertise as much as I do your friendship.

I've had the privilege of working closely with three University of Dayton presidents — Brother Ray Fitz, Dan Curran and Eric Spina. Each in his own way models what it means to lead with a servant's heart. I can never repay you for your trust and faith in me.

"Posties of a certain era" — my lifelong journalism friends from Ohio University — continually inspire me with their curiosity, compassion and love for a compelling story. We're carrying each other through the pandemic, one Zoom call at a time. Special thanks to John Batteiger, Chris Celek, Julie Fanselow, Jeff Grabmeier, Robin Hepler, Theresa Hitchens, Scott Johnson, Peggy Loftus, Alan Miller, Larry Neumeister, Peg O'Laughlin, Anne Saker, Bill Schulz and Scott Stephens. A couple of the writings in this book hark way back to my days as managing editor of *The Post*, OU's daily student newspaper.

What can I say about my college roommates, Denise Summers and Toni Clarkson? You're family — and always will be.

Huge thanks to my creative sidekick Anna Lefler for your endless encouragement and generous heart. From helping me make my prose stronger to making me laugh at life's absurdities, you are the friend we all need in our corner.

And to all my friends who responded with a resounding "yes!" when I told them I was writing a book, I'm infinitely grateful for your support, especially Nancy Berk, Ellen Belcher, Tim Bete, Patricia Wynn Brown, Bob Daley, Mickey Dickman, Fran Evans, Mark Fisher, Bev and Bob Gallagher, Vicki Giambrone, Kate Harrison, Emily Holterman, Sharon Howard, Diana Kiser, Lisa Kloppenberg, Shannon Miller, Kate Mulcahy, Allia Zobel Nolan, Elaine Opper, Jeaneen Parsons, Linda Robertson, Marcia Stewart, Bob Taft and Teresa Zumwald.

My love and gratitude goes out to the Bombeck family and the writing community who helped to build the Erma Bombeck Writers' Workshop into a national treasure. You inspire me with your belief in what's possible.

For my roots, I'm grateful to my siblings — Mike, Nancy and Tim — and the St. Chris Class of 1972.

Finally, to my family in Pakistan and other far-flung places in the world, thank you for welcoming me with love and acceptance — and allowing me to carry a notebook to weddings and excursions. A few pieces from our family's trips to Pakistan were published in *USA Today, The Christian Science Monitor, The Guardian* (London) and the *Dayton Daily News.*

Most of all, all my love to the Rizvi men (and our bonus daughter Alaina). You're amazing in every way.

About the Author

Teri Rizvi is the founder and director of the Erma Bombeck Writers' Workshop at the University of Dayton, where she serves as executive director of strategic communications. Her essays and feature stories have appeared in *USA Today*, *The Christian Science Monitor*, *The Guardian* (London), *University of Dayton Magazine* and the *Dayton Daily News*, among other print and online media.

She is the co-editor of *Laugh Out Loud: 40 Women Humorists Celebrate Then and Now … Before We Forget* and *Sisters! Bonded by Love and Laughter*, a humor book that celebrates the bond of sisters (and soul sisters), both published in conjunction with the Erma Bombeck Writers' Workshop. Her essay "Living in the Moment" will appear in *Fast Fierce Women* (Woodhall Press, 2022).